ISESAKI, JAPAN

Voices
FROM THE
MIDDLE
BOOK 2

THE WORLD IS OUR BLOG

Authors & Artists

SPRINGFIELD, MISSOURI MIDDLE SCHOOLS

SONSHIP
PRESS

Sonship Press, Springfield, MO 65807

VOICES FROM THE MIDDLE
BOOK 2

Copyright © 2007

ISBN: 978-0-9779535-3-0

Visit: www.sonshipbooks.com

Cover Design: Keith Locke
Book Design: Terry White

2131 W. Republic Rd., PMB 41, Springfield, MO 65807

DEDICATION

This book is dedicated to our friends in Isesaki, Japan.

Editorial Staff

Alison Bickers
Adam Crawford
Austin Lamb
Rachel Lucht
Katherine Mellenbruch
Nikki Nowak
Nick Orlando
Jayne Rey
Matt Vierkant
Annie Webber

CONTENTS

Stain Glass - Kori Chrismer (Art)
Dreams - Brandon Cole (Art)

STUDY MIDDLE SCHOOL

My Mom - Trinity McCroskey
The Boy Break Up - Brittany Hurt
Winter Night - Regan Fink
Gone - Racheal Hawthorne
My Experience with Diabetes - Nora Key
My Biggest Flashback - Lacey Arner
The Kingdom - Kevin Robb
Kathy's Stroke - Destiny Kidd
Breaking Arms - Jackie Bradley
Hank Aaron - Colin Wilson
Life Told How It Is - Brittany Hurt
Friends - Andrew Choate
My Dad - Amanda Powers
Brittany, Accident Princess - Lacey Arner
That Boy - Chari Heard
Wipe Out - Alexandra Tinsley
The Terrible Ship - Alexis Bond
Winter - Thao Van
Forbidden Street - Rachel Staudte
Someone I'll Never Forget - Tara Wood
Adjustments - Kaitlyn Seats
MOM - Adam Carr
Life Goes On.... - Racheal Hawthorne
Grandpa's Field - Randy Bradshaw
I Don't Know Why - Janessa McCafferty
Moonlit Pond - Kristain Marsh
Deserted Highway - Jessica DeMalia
Saturday - Jessica DeMalia
Normandy - Chris Haller
Deal With It - Jenna Roan

FOREWORD

The word is the essence of expression—voice. It houses a world of meaning and conveys the most heart-felt perspectives. The voices in this second edition of middle school reflections include writings from students in Isesaki, Japan. The adult world knows, but forgets in its own issues, that adolescence is fraught with the internal wars of physical and emotional turmoil compounded by the external drama of life in a myriad of contexts—personal or global. Again, students voice their opinions or frustrations or share experiences that teach, impact, uplift, or warm the heart. Some step into the world of fantasy. The non-fiction world is hardly the same one as it was generations ago. Stability from anywhere is increasingly illusive. Young people have futures, but their own voices betray the overwhelming sense that they feel alone in trying to figure out where or how they will fit into society.

The companion to voice is the ear of compassion. Listening should be our goal as readers. Extending hope to each other through understanding, will be our creative response.

How do you follow a class act? Of course, the performance must be bigger and better! Such is the case with the second edition of *Voices from the Middle*. This time around, the voices are heard from so many good schools in Springfield (thanks to "extra-mile" kind of teachers), and even from far away Isesaki, Japan. We are indebted to Carrol Lund, teacher of Japanese at Kickapoo High School, for her hard work in contacting our Sister City for submissions from middle school students, and for co-translating the work with Toru Motosu from Isesaki once it arrived. In Japan, calligraphy samples are considered as important as writing samples.

Reading and appreciating the minds and hearts from cultures other than our own is one way to communicate a positive message. We are together in the need to understand each other and build on creative ways to bring harmony and peace to our world. Young people in any culture deal with the pressure from within at the same time as they deal with momentous pressures in their societies. The ability to express all of these hopes and fears is a step toward self-acceptance and a step toward figuring out their roles in the future.

Students who have written for "Voices" and many who have not will be in places of leadership in our countries in the not-too-distant future.

—**Barbara Kraft**

INTRODUCTION

EXPLANATION OF THE JAPANESE MIDDLE SCHOOL SYSTEM

At the time these Japanese entries were solicited and sent to us, Isesaki, Japan (Springfield's Sister City SINCE 1988) had six junior high schools. On January 1, 2005, Isesaki merged with three nearby communities and now has 11 junior highs. The six schools that are included in Voices from the Middle II are Daiichi JHS with 503 students, Daini JHS with 615, Daisan JHS with 654, Daiyon JHS with 604 students, Uehasu JHS with 613 students, and Miyago JHS with a student enrollment of 694 students. Japanese junior high schools are designed for students in 7th grade (ichi-nensei), 8th grade (ni-nensei), and 9th grade (san-nensei).The children's ages range from 13 years old to 15 years old. All students in Isesaki wear school uniforms designated by the school.

The school week is Monday through Friday. The Japanese school year begins in April and is organized on a trimester system. Compulsory education in Japan is nine years: six years in elementary schools and three in junior high schools. Almost all students go to high school. Some students go to schools in Isesaki others go to schools out side the area. Entrance exams are a requirement for entry into high school. One cannot enter high school if the exam is not passed. Ninth graders study very hard in order to pass the exams. Exam season starts in January and extends to March. Winter is a very busy season for junior high students.

Junior high students participate in after school club activities. Activities never interrupt the school day. Clubs range from a variety of sports such as ping pong or base-ball to a variety of cultural activities such as tea ceremony or flower arranging. Most students belong to their select-ed club for all three years of junior high. Students can not belong to more than two clubs.

Japan has a National Ministry of Education (Monbushoo) that determines curriculum and textbooks. Literacy rate in the country is over 99% even though liter-acy requires mastery of three different character sets: hira-gana, katakana, and 1950 kanji. Japanese is classified as a level four difficulty language for native speakers of English. French and Spanish are level one difficulty. Kickapoo and Glendale High Schools in Springfield offer Japanese language instruction.

Thanks to Springfield's strong Sister City relation-ship, two select students from each of Isesaki's junior highs have visited Springfield for a week in August since

1988. Originally the student group came each year. Now our routine is that the Isesaki Junior High students visit Springfield on the odd years and Springfield high school students experience Japan through Japan Study Tour on the even years. This collaboration of Voices from the Middle II represents a high point in the already strong sister city relationship.

DAISAN
MIDDLE
SCHOOL

My School Bag—Marie Tanba

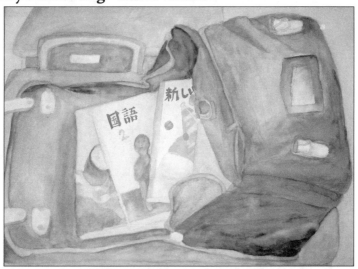

THE JAPANESE BOOKBAG

Each school has its designated book bag as well as its uniform. Families buy the selected bags at the shops designated by the schools. The price is about 3000 yen (approximately $30). All book bags are designed in a specific size and the classroom desks have special hooks to uniformly hang the bag. Most of the students' textbooks are slim and paper back. The Japanese book bags therefore do not need to be as unwieldly as American book bags.

UEHASU MIDDLE SCHOOL

I Am Not Strange

There is one thing I always wonder about. Almost all girls dislike their fathers during their rebellious stage, but I do not understand those girls. I wonder why they think their fathers are weird. I have thought before, "Am I strange?" But I definitely say I am not.

Fathers work for their families everyday. So does my father. He is a truck driver. He leaves home at three o'clock in the morning and gets home at 9:00 in the evening. Sometimes it is 10:00 or 11:00 when he gets home. I am proud of him when I see him exhausted. Even though he is very tired, he goes to work everyday. I know he is so tired. My mother works, too. She is an office worker and she works on Saturdays and Sundays. On weekends, my father does housework. Of course, my brother and I help him. My family helps each other.

So, I do not understand why other girls cannot stand

their fathers. My mother often asks me how I feel toward my father. I respond that I do not at all feel as other girls do. She once told me that there was a time when she used to dislike her father. She often rejected him, but I do not have a slight feeling like that. My father works for us everyday. He would be hurt if I felt like other girls do toward their fathers. Thinking of that, I of course would not say anything. It is not just for now, but I will never think badly of him.

I want to be proud of him even if my friends think their fathers are weird. I would not say, "thank you," face to face, but I want to express my feelings. I want to help my father and my mother more and I want to ease their burden.

I still do not understand why girls think negatively about their fathers. But I will not think I am strange since I do not dislike him. I am what I am regardless of how other girls feel. I can say that I will never hate him. I cannot say anything to him, but I am very proud and thankful of him. I want to take care of him. My heart is full of appreciation.

—Sayaka Kuroda
Uehasu Junior High

父親について   私は変じゃない

　私は疑問に思うことがあります。ほとんどの女の子は、反抗期からかお父さんをイヤがる時期があります。でも、私には分かりません。なぜお父さんをイヤがるのか。そんな私は変なのかなあ。と時々思う事がありました。でもやっぱり変ではないと思います。

　　お父さんは毎日毎日、私達家族のために働いてお金を稼いで来てくれています。私のお父さんもそうです。私のお父さんは、

トラックの運転手をしています。夜中の三時に家を出て、帰ってくる
のは、いつも夜の九時です。遅い時は十時や十一時にもなります。
そんなに働いてヘトヘトになって帰ってくるお父さんを私は誇り
に思います。どんなに疲れていても休む事なく毎日仕事に行きます。
本当は、すごくつらいと思います。

　　　私の家はお母さんも働いています。お母さんは事務員で
働いていて土、日も休みはありません。そこで、その土、日はお父さん
が家の家事をしています。もちろん私達兄弟も手伝っています。そうして
私の家族は助け合って暮らしています。そうしてがんばっている
お父さんをイヤがる気持か私には分かりません。

　　　お母さんによく聞かれます、「お父さんイヤじゃないの？」
って。でも私は普通に答えました。「イヤじゃないよ」って。

　　　お母さんは私くらいの年ごろにお父さんをイヤがっていた

年ごろがあったと話を聞いた事があります。「イヤ」とか「きたない
からやめて」とかよく言っていたそうです。でも私は毎日がんばって
働いてくれているお父さんをそう思った事はありません。がんばって
働いているのにそれも家族のためなのにイヤなんて言ったらお父さん
がどんなに傷付く事になるのだろうか。そう考えるとやっぱりイヤと
は思えません。それはきっと今だけではないと思います。この先ずっと
そう思っていられたらいいなあ、と思います。　もしも周りの友達
がそうなってしまっても私はずっとお父さんを誇りに思っていたい、と
思いました。毎日毎日、働いているお父さんに直接「ありがとう」なんて
言えないけど態度で表現できたらいいなあ、と思います。

　　　今まで以上にお手伝いをして、お父さんとお母さんを
少しでも楽にさせる事ができるように私なりに努力したいと思います。

お父さんをイヤなんてなぜ思うのかは私には、まだ分かりません。
お父さんをイヤがらない私は変なのかなとは、もう一度も思いません。
周りの子がどう思っても私は私のままだと思います。お父さんをイヤ
がる事はないと思います。毎日毎日がんばって働いているお父さんに
普段は何も言えないけど本当は誇りに思う気持ちと感謝の気持ちで
いっぱいです。これからも体に気を付けて毎日がんばってほしいと
思います。本当にお父さんには感謝の気持ちでいっぱいです。

Getting Through

"I have hands and legs, and I can see through my eyes and hear through my ears." What would you think if you were told that? "It is the way things are," is so easy to say. How would you answer if asked, "Have you ever thought of people who are unable to do so?"

In this world, there are disabled people. Some of them are disabled from birth, others from accident or disease. There are many kinds of disabled people. Some cannot see or use their hands or legs properly. They are not what they wanted to be. Many people still do not understand that they are not special. I was one of them who did not understand.

When I was an elementary school child, my family and I attended an event for disabled people. At that time I did not have any images of them and said to my parents, "that guy is a weirdo." I wonder if one of them had heard what I said. It would have hurt their human rights.

Some have such serious disabilities. For example, people who cannot have conversations with others, people who have to stay in bed all the time. But I think everyone has his own heart and feelings even if he is unable to speak or if he is bedridden. My mother once told me that when we speak to them, they express their feelings by their faces and not by words. If they are depressed, they express with their depressed faces. If they are happy, they express with a smile. I felt so happy when I heard this story. Before that, I had heard that they would not answer us when we spoke to them, so it made us feel sad. But we can communicate with each other when we talk to each other deliberately.

If you were disabled, you would feel sorry if someone spoke ill of your handicap. You would feel sorry even if you were not that disabled one. So, you should not say, "that guy is a weirdo," like I said before. If you think that to be true, you should think it over again. Handicapped people have hearts and feelings just like you do. We change our image of the disabled when we understand them and communicate with them as we do with other people.

I still do not understand perfectly, and I do not know if my thoughts are correct or not. But I have one thing in mind: with understanding and considering the disabled the same as other people, the wall that separates people will collapse. We will be able to communicate through heart and feelings. As my mother did, it is important to teach people who do not understand. The world would be full of smiles if many people understood each other.

I will learn much more about disabled people. I want to put this in my mind: Everyone is the same even if disabled. We can communicate.
—Marie Ishihara
Uehasu Middle School

心や気持ちが通じ合う時

「今、私には手があり足があり、目も見えて耳も聞こえている。」
もし、こんなことを言われたら、あなたはどう思うだろうか。「そんな
こと当たり前。」こうしてすませることならかんたんにできる。それ
ならば、「その当たり前のことができない人がいるのを考えたことが
あるか」と聞かれたら、どう答えるだろう。

　この世の中には障害というものを持つ人がいる。それは
生まれながらというのもあれば、事故や病気が原因というのもある。
目が目なかったり、手足が満足に使えなかったり、その種類は数多い。
だが、障害は持ちたくて持っているわけではない。それに、持って
いるからといって特別な人ではないということを、まだ理解できて
いない人は多くいる。　私も理解できていない中の一人だった。

　私が小学生の頃、休みの日に家族で出かけた時に、障害を
持つ人達と一緒に参加するイベントへ行ったことがあった。その
頃の私は障害というものをまったく理解できていなくて、つい、親に
向かって、「あの人、おかしいね。」と言ってしまった。もしあの
言葉が本にんの耳に入っていたら。今考えると、あきらかにその人
の人権を傷つけてしまう言葉だったと思う。

　障害にはとても重いものもある。例えば、脳に障害があり、
人との会話ができない人、ずっと寝たきりになってしまう人だ。
でも、会話ができなくても、寝たきりになっていても、心や自分
の気持ちは誰にでも必ずあると私は思う。前に母が話してくれたが、
重度な障害、会話ができないような人でも、こちらが何が話しかけると、
言葉じゃなく表情で伝えてくれるという。　嫌な時は嫌な表情で、嬉しい

時は嬉しい表情で。私はそれを聞いてとても嬉しく思った。　今まで
はよく重度な障害を持っている人は話しかけても言葉を返してくれなくて、
だんだんむなしい気持ちになってくると聞いたが、よく相手と
向き合って話していれば、きっと気持ちは通じ合えるのだ。

　　だが、心や気持ちはとても繊細だ。ちょっとしたことでも傷
つきやすい。まして、自分の持つ障害や嫌な所を言われればとても
辛い思いをするだろう。それは障害を持っていてもいなくても同じ
ことだ。だから、前に私が言ってしまったように、「あの人、おかしい
ね。」のような言葉は決して言ってはならない。もし、おかしいと
思ったとしても、よく考えてみるといい。その人のどこかい障害が
あるだけで、あとの心や気持ちはみんな同じ人なのだ。障害を持つ
人のことをよく理解した上で、みんな同じ人としてふれ合えば、きっと
障害という感覚を乗り越えることができると思う。

　　私は、まだ障害というものを全て理解できているわけではない。
だから、自分が考えていることが正しいかどうかは分からない。だが、
一つだけ自分なりにはっきり言えることがある。それは、障害を
持つ人のことを理解して、みんな同じ人として生きていけば、障害
という間の壁がなくなり、みんなの心や気持ちが通じ合えるということ
だ。　母のように理解している人が理解していない人に対して広める
ことが大切である。一人でも多くの人が障害について理解してくれれば、
きっと世の中が明るく笑顔になるだろう。

　　これから私は少しずつでも、障害についての理解を深めたいと
思う。そして時々思い出したい。　障害があってもみんな同じ人であり、
きっと心や気持ちは通じ合うと。

DAINI MIDDLE SCHOOL

Life

Have you ever thought about life? Have you thought about how happy your life is? I feel that the number of people who want to die is increasing. Actually, I was one of those people who was thinking of dying, but the following event changed my thinking.

Last year I lost my dear dog. He came to my house when I was a little girl. The veterinarian told me that he would not live long since he was premature. But seeing him run and jump in my house, I would not think about that. He gave me the power to live. He was a friendly boy and liked people. He often messed around with clean clothes and scratched the toilet sheets. My mom always got mad at him. But when I was depressed or crying, he was always next to me. He looked as if he was cheering me up. I did not have a slight thought about what I was told about him.

On December 23rd, ten days before his 10th birthday, he closed his nine year and eleven month life. We did not know the name of the disease. We were told it was a nerve virus. I thought that he had died of old age. I did not notice a change in his body when I saw him still running and jumping. He had been losing his teeth and he could not eat hard foods. At last he threw up foods, even water. Even though he could not open his mouth or move, he tried to go to the food plate and eat. I felt so sorry since he looked like he was telling us that he wanted to live and could live longer.

On the last day, he looked as if he were waiting for my family to come back. My mother said, "Ok, you had a great life, ok," looking at the pitiful boy. My mother's words eased him. He breathed deeply and did not move any longer though his eyes were still open. But his heart was beating and then he stopped breathing. My tears did not stop falling, I looked at him and he tried to live to the last moment. My whole family cried. I had never seen my father cry before. Our dog was so precious to us. I have never thought about life deeply. Now I know how hard a time it is to lose my precious things.

There is one thing I had in mind after his death. We are not alone. I used to think that I am alone or I am the only girl who had a hard time. But this is a self-centered view. It is proof that I had not seen my surroundings. There are always friends and teachers who will listen to me, and my family is there to give me support. We are living in these circumstances. I feel ashamed of myself that I thought I was alone.

Living is wonderful. Everything is not always good, sometimes we worry and want to give up. But we have our lives. I want everybody to think about our lives.

It is hard to express my thought in words, but one

thing I can say is that life is wonderful. Chatting with friends, singing favorite songs from TV—feeling these things means that we are happy. If you are tired of your life, I do not want you to give up. I want to say to everyone, "It is wonderful that you live and that you can live."

Thank you very much.

—Erika Uchida

Daini Middle School, Isesaki, Japan

生きるということ

みなさんは生きるということについて、考えたことがありますか。生きるということがどんなに幸せか考えたことがありますか。　私は今「死にたい」と思っている人が増えている気がします。実際に私も思っていた頃がありました。けれど、そう思うことをやめる出来事がありました。

去年、大事な飼犬を亡くしました。わたしがまだ幼い頃。その犬は私の家に来ました。獣医さんに診てもらったところ「未熟児で他の犬ほど長くは生きられない」と言われました。けれど、家の中で元気に走り回る飼犬を見て、そんなことは気にならなかったし、元気に動く姿は私にとって元気の素となりました。

人と接するのが大好きな人なつこい犬でした。たまに、たたんだ洗濯物をあちこちにもっていったり、トイレのミートを引っかいたりなどのいたずらをして、母に怒られていました。でも、私が辛い時や泣いてる時はいつもそばにいて、まるで私をなぐさめるようにじっとそばで座っていてくれました。だから「長く生きられない」なんて言われたことなどすっかり忘れていました。

十歳の誕生日を十日後にひかれた十一月二十二日、九年と

十一カ月の短い命を終えました。病名はあいませんでした。何かの
ウィルスが神経の中に入ったとしか伝えられませんでした。　私は
寿命かと思っていましたが、急激な飼い犬の死に言葉がでません
でした。歩き方が少しのろくなったり、歯が抜けて固いものが
食べられなくなったりしたけれど、相変わらず走り回っていたので体
の変化に気がつきませんでした。とうとうエサも水も吐いてしまいました。
けれど、口が開かなくなって動けない状態なのに、エサの置いてある
所まで何度も倒ぞながら歩いて行くのです。その姿は「生きたい
まだ生きられる」と言っているように見えてとても辛かったです。

　　　最後の日は家族が帰ってくるのを待っていたかのように見えました。
とても苦しんでる様子に母が「もういいよ、がんばったんだから。もう
いいよ」　と声をかけました。その言葉に安心したかのように、大きく
息を吸い込んで、眼を見開いたまま動かなくなりました。でも、呼吸
が止まっても心臓は動いていました。最後まで生きようとする姿を
見て、涙がとまりませんでした。家族みんな泣いてたけど、私は父が
声をあげて泣くのを初めて見たので驚きました。飼い犬はそのくらい
家族にとって大切な存在だったのだなと思いました。

　　　私は今までに生きるということについて深く考えたことは
なかったけれど、自分の大切なものを失うということがどんなに辛い
ことか、分かった気がします。それと同時に、命のあるものはどんな
に辛くても、最後のその瞬間には「生きたい」と願うものなのでは
ないかと思いました。

　　　私はこのことがあってから思うことがあります。人は一人じゃ
ないのだなということです。私はよく「どうせ一人ぼっちだ」とか
「私だけがイヤな思いをしている」などと思っていました。それは

自分中心の考えであって、周りが見えていなかった証拠だと思います。周りにはいつでも相談にのってくれる友達、先生、そいていつもそばで支えてくれている家族がいます。その中で私たちは生きているのです。なのに一人だと思っていた自分ははずかしいと思いました。

　生きているということは、すばらしいと思います。人生の中で全てがみないいことではないけれど、悩んで、辛くなって、投げだしたくなる気持ちもあってこそ、今私たちは生きているのではないかと思います。私は生きることについてみんなに考えてほしいのです。

　あまり上手く言い表すことはできないけれど、ただ一つ言えることは「生きられる」ということはすばらしいということです。友達と何気ない話で笑い合うこと、思いがけずテレビから大好きな曲が流れ、思わず口ずさむこと。それらを感じられることは幸せだということです。生きることにつかえても、決して生きることをあきらめてほしくないのです。

　私は今生きているすべての人にいいたいです。「生きるということ、生きられるということはすばらしいことなんだ」と。御静聴ありがとうございました。

内田えりか

Makoto (Faith)—Mai Tsukui

DAIICHI MIDDLE SCHOOL

Only Fifteen

At first I thought adulthood begins at twenty, but this would mean that on your birthday everyone simply transforms from a child into an adult. I have a sister who is 21 and I thought she was an adult. But then I heard my mother scolding her. Does this mean that she is still a child?

So, being an adult must be more than just being a certain age. It must be something that adults do; something new and different, maybe something like smoking, drinking, or voting. Though, even these things do not seem to separate women from girls. If, for example, smoking meant that you were grown up, then many of my teenage friends would be considered adults. If it means drinking, then my father would still be a child, since he does not drink. As for voting, recently 50% of people turned out on election day to cast their vote. What about the other 50%? Because of this are they no longer considered adults?

So now I think that adulthood is not about special privileges or activities, but rather it is about something more basic and personal. It must be who you are rather than what you do. Adulthood must have something to do with simply living a good and manageable life. This means we are not magically adults on our twentieth birthday, but become mature over time.

The dictionary defines adulthood as being something which is only about how old you are, but I have come to believe that the maturity of your mind is more important, whatever your age. Today I am 15 years old, not yet an adult by any standard. Even though my parents are surprised that I grew up so fast, they are quick to tell me that I am only 15. Still only a child, but also a child ready to grow up.

In my life, I want to try many new things, meet many different people, and experience all that the world has to offer. This will allow me to gain maturity and learn how to live the best possible life I can. Then, one day, I will finally be able to say that I am an adult.

—Azusa Osawa
Daiichi Middle School, Isesaki, Japan

This entry was originally written in English, not Japanese, for an English writing contest. Legal age in Japan is twenty.

Zoa Gongen Ritsuzo (Temple Guardian)
Koyama Saki

MIYAGON
MIDDLE
SCHOOL

Kingfisher—Takaaki Otani
Kingfisher is beautiful
From his head to his toe
His beautiful color
His style of flying
His shining color
No body beats him...

かわせみ　　　　大谷天誠

かわせみは、きれい
すみからすみまで。
あのきれいな色
あの飛びかた、
色の輝き
かなう鳥は
い、い、い

The People of Darkness—Rei Shimizu

> The twilight makes the blue sky darken
> Appearing one by one
> The people of the darkness
> Stars and moon

闇の住人　清水玲
青空が
夕暮れ見えて
暗くなる
ぽつりぽつりと
姿を見せる
闇の住人
星や月

DAIYON
MIDDLE
SCHOOL

Seabird—Aya Nakajima

CARVER
MIDDLE
SCHOOL

Why Won't You Love Me?
> Don't know where to start,
> Don't know how to end,
> Not sure what to say
> Not sure how to act.
> Tell me what to do,
> Show me where to go.
> Be my light
> Be my tunnel
> Be my beginning, middle, and end.
> Be everything, nothing, anything!
> Just be with me!

> How can you trust me?
> One, two, three,
> I'm out!
> How about a re-roll?
> Maybe 4 times a charm?
> Is there love at first sight?

Or is it just imagining?
Shouldn't it be feelings?
Shouldn't it be happiness?
Can't it be me and you?

I have learned,
And I have cleansed.
I am your wheat,
I know no chaff.
I can repent,
I will repent,
If you'll let me.

Open Your heart,
Let me in!
Why won't you love me?

Your smile,
Your laugh,
Your hair,
Your smell,
YOU!
You drive me crazy
You won't let me sleep,
Your beauty makes me turn,
Then I fade into exhaustion.

One deep sigh,
And one great thought
I am in Dreamworld,
Fantasy Land,
And I'm with you.

—Robert Schaeffer

"Violence" in Carver

Earlier in the year, our class spoke about violence and fights here at our school. In this discussion I was unusually quiet and I didn't interject any of my opinions. But what I listened to slightly, though not too much, surprised me.

Lots of kids in the class spoke of how they fought with others at school as if it was an everyday aspect. They said things like," talking it out never works," "I don't like peer mediation" and "fighting is fun." This got me thinking about things like how immature is it to fight all the time... and like it.

Recently we wrote letters to people fighting for us and for the things we believe in. How could anyone write to them respectfully and then go to school and smack someone because they called them something bad.

This reminds me of how my brother and I used to fight. We'd fight over where to sit at dinner or what show to watch on TV. We did this everyday over the stupidest stuff. Now we've grown out of such idiocy, and to think, now 13 year olds are acting like toddlers. It's insane.

Perhaps I shouldn't have been so shocked to know this about my fellow students, but I believe we can be more mature.

—Loren Casteel

My Dad

When one of your friends loses a parent you really can't understand what they're going through, unless you have been there yourself. That's what happened to me. My best friend, the one person that I cared about so much, was gone in a flash. My father, Tony Helsel, died of liver failure on July 26, 2002, while I was at a baseball game.

My dad was always there when I needed him, and he had hundreds of friends. He was forty when he died. I was only ten. While I was at the baseball game that night, the Lord told me my father was with him now, and I knew he had passed away. Right before my team took the field, I burst out in tears, in front of everyone. Grown men were crying when they got to the visitation later that week.

My family also had a dog named Murphy. He and Dad would always hang around in the lunch-lounger (a chair that could fit lunch around it). My dad loved that dog. Almost every day, Murphy would escape, and then come back later. My dad would always say, "That dog better die after me, or else I'll be crushed!"

Well, that's the way it went. Two days after my father died, so did my dog. Perhaps the separation was too much for Murphy. They were both cremated and buried together. That way, my dad and Murphy would always be together, even in Heaven.

—Colton Helsel

My Lifesaver

When you hear the word "lifesaver," what comes to mind? Maybe a fruity candy or a round floatation device, or maybe even an angel. I think of my best friend, Molly.

Before Molly, I had never had a true best friend. You know, someone you could tell everything to and they would tell you everything back. I have always been a true best friend, but the friends I chose used me, talked behind my back, stole my things, and tried to change me into what my mom called "not a nice little girl." The friends that I had chosen made all the wrong decisions before they made the right ones. Some of them still have not made the right decisions, like one of my best friends in elementary school. She started middle school at Carver in 6th grade like the rest of us, scared, timid, and confused. We still talked but weren't "friends." We hung out with different crowds. I am kind of glad because if we had stayed friends, no telling where I would be right now.

Then I met Molly in the summer between 5th and 6th grades. We became friends, not best friends yet though. She thought I was annoying and outspoken. I thought she was the best thing that ever happened to me and later I learned I was right. Most of my friends and I grew apart, but Molly and I grew together. She still thinks that I am annoying and outspoken, but in a different way. It's true— I still think Molly is the best thing that ever happened to me. She taught me what it's like to have a true best friend, to love a friend like a sister. Molly is my lifesaver, my angel, my best friend. She truly saved my life because only God knows where I would have ended up.

—Hannah Rowan

Hate/ Love

My life is insane. Everyone thinks of me as a spastic, weird, kind of cool, crazy 14 years old. But really I'm a spastic, weird, kinda cool crazy 13 year-old. For real, I'm just depressed and have no other way to express myself, so I do the craziest things. I mean, you only live once, right? Well, I let people see whatever they want in me because I don't care. If they ever see the real me or my life story, they would feel so bad. That's kind of why I stopped caring. Most people misjudge me, so I do not show who I really am. I am just crazy.

Some ways to be misjudged are hateful ways. No one should hate anyone. But still they do. Chances are you could love the people you hate. So get to know people better. In a weird sense kind of forget about everything you know and try again on your own judgment. Just walk in their shoes. Then in the end you'll see I'm right. Maybe crazy, maybe not.

—Nick Leach

Waiting

Here I lie on soft grass waiting for you to come back. Devastation fills my heart, as it grows darker and darker. I call for you, hoping you are close by, but, of course, you are not. You have forgotten, as always; I have wasted my important time. Waiting for nothing. I once loved you...not any more. I've lost so much trust for human kind because of you.

The garden has blackened now. The biting cold has come. I try desperately to find shelter. I'm coaxed by sweet roses sent to stay in the open. The roses whose thorns have grown too strong have snatched my unprotected heart. Finally I'm let go, dropped, relieved but afraid. Afraid of the thorns, grabbing my exposed soul.

For a long time the garden which I have once loved is forgotten. The same way I have been forgotten. The spring and summer comes, the roses are pulled from the garden. I can now return. The sweet smell of honey-suckles fills the warm air. The overwhelming scent sends me falling into a deep sleep. I dream of my memories of your love. Then I see the honeysuckles; there is hope. I feel so alive, but I must remember what happened last time. So, I stay away, but the honeysuckle smell grows stronger and stronger all the while hugging me closer and closer. Now I am free of

regret, safe from all roses, and hugged and properly loved by
the honeysuckles.

—Giulia Rusciano

Fear
I am not scared of the dark,
Or of a big dog's bark,
I do not fear the fact of dying,
Although you thought I was lying,
Honestly, I don't have many fears,
Except the few that bring me to tears,
Like am I alone, or on my own?
I never again want to feel hate,
For once I want to feel safe.

These four walls are my prison. Will you even listen?
What happens to people? Do they hide?
Is that the percentage of this nation's suicide?

I need so much therapy, will they be able to see
And say what's so wrong with me?
But as they search for an answer that could be found,
Might as well drop here and lie face down on the ground.

If you were to look at my life for a second,
You'd think I had the perfect life,
But take another look and you'll see,
That in my palm lies a knife.

And as I search for some reason
I look around; I have nothing to believe in.

—Tyler Foreman

Echoes
The place. The animal pound.
The dark, damp place where little or no light shines.
The echoes droning, never ending,
Making one go into a crazy
Madness of sorrow for the animals.
The bars, the cages. Not fitting in.
No warmth, just cold, damp darkness.
Barely alive. The animals whose
Evil owners left them or just didn't care.
Now they're in here, this infinite
Darkness. For those who are lucky,
They will see the light again, but the
Unfortunate ones will meet their end in this horrid,
 Never-ending eternity
Of cold, evil darkness.
Not even enough food to thrive.
The only sounds
You hear are the droning, droning echoes.
The animals whispering to the
Cold, cold darkness with their voices fading
As their breath of life does
Also. Their only chance of life is to hope.
Hope for every little minute, second,
And day.
Week after week, never fading, never ending hope.
The never
Ending screaming, tearing hope.
But alas, when hope is broken,
The animal is gone.
New animals time to experience the droning, droning
Echoes in this never lightening,
Ever darkening tormenting hole that

Buries itself in the animals heart
And soul and slowly torments and
Destroys the poor, poor creature.
But the suffering shall end with light or darkness.
On the Third Avenue in the city of nowhere,
Where no person is there, yet everyone is.
On the edge of the world yet not even on this planet.
In this horrible place, the keeper of echoes,
The absorber of sound,
In this place of silence only echoes can be heard.

—Jacob Beckham

Back to Reality

Many people think that there is such a thing as a perfect society. They believe that there is a possible system of governing people that would please the people. However, I think that these people need to come back to the real world. There is no way of keeping people content. One might ask, why?

The answer is simple; it can be summed up in a single word: men. For man is corrupt. Man has a desire for worldly things, material objects, and above all else, power. Power is what man will do about anything to possess. Men will lie, steal, cheat, and do a number of things if it is to their advantage.

That is one of the reasons why dictatorships often turn into tyrannies, why egalitarian societies sometimes turn into dictatorships. Even with men who try to keep the people's interests in mind. Marx, Hitler, Mussolini, there are a number of people who created governments with hopes of making things better. Yet, from Marx came communism, a twisted rendition of what he originally intended. Hitler strove for power; he wanted to rule the world. Mussolini was a tyrant, but he began with the intentions of making a better government. Even democracy has its flaws. Perfection in society is a fool's hope. Those who try to form a perfect utopian society should come to reality.

—Christian Cook

A Moment in Time

On May 13, 2003 my mom, brothers, and I were taking my little brother to preschool.

We were in the turning lane and as we were turning....

"Oh my God! Mommy! Mommy! I can't get out!"

"Kayleen, kids wake up! Are you ok?"

"I can't get out! My seat belt is on! My door is locked! What do I do?"

I realized my mom was fine and trying to get my brothers, Matt and Brandon, out of the car.

The ambulance screamed up. The paramedics told my mom to move out of the way so that they could take my brothers out of the car. Next thing I noticed was that my brothers were burned. My little brother, Brandon, was yelling for the family. My older brother Matt was bleeding and the paramedics were putting a tube down his throat so that he could breathe. He was unconscious.

They were rushed to St. John's Hospital. Then my dad arrived. He saw Matt and Brandon and dropped to his knees because he thought my mom and I died at the scene of the accident. The chaplin said, "We need to talk."

My dad found out that our family survived. "Thank you, Lord. You saved my family."

Later, I went to the hospital because I wanted to see my brothers. As I was walking up to see Matt, I got scared.

I got into his room and I wanted to talk to him, but I couldn't do it. My mom took me out to the hallway; I was crying. That night we got the news that Matt was going to St. Louis Children's Hospital.

Many months later, Matt is still going through surgeries and will continue them for the rest of his life. Even though he will have those surgeries, I am very thankful that my family is still alive today.

I really do love my brothers!

—Kayleen Gravelin

Thanks to My Anonymous Rescuer

It was a Thursday night in July. My friend Marina and I were excited about the Murphy Lee concert we would be attending later that night. When we finally arrived at the concert there weren't many people there yet. So we got really close to the front. Then as it got later, more people began to pile up in the small area reserved for the listeners. Soon I was surrounded by people, all of whom smelled as if they hadn't bathed in months.

I began to feel sick as more and more people crowded around me. The smoke blowing in my face didn't help much, and I soon realized that if I didn't escape from this madness for at least a few minutes, there would be messy consequences. So I made my first mistake; I told my friend to wait there to keep our front row spots while I tried to make my way toward the bathrooms, which seemed to be miles away through all the people. So my journey began.

I angered many people as I pushed my way through them as politely as possible. I received many unhappy glares as I disturbed conversations between small groups of people. Finally, after being pushed and yelled at many times, I reached the bathrooms. I looked out at the anxious crowd impatiently awaiting Murphy Lee's arrival. I was happy to be out of the rambunctious crowd.

As I was in the restroom regrouping, I heard the whole crowd start to cheer, and then the music began. It was the opening for Murphy Lee. My heart sank; I knew getting back through the mob was going to be a nightmare, with all the excitement of the music. And then the nightmare began.

The first couple of yards were not so bad; it seemed the people in the back were the ones who didn't want to dance, so it was pretty easy. But as I moved on deeper into the crowd, it got worse, as the unpleasantly familiar dirty looks returned, but that wasn't the worst of it by any means. The closer I got to the front, the more furious the people became. Then, as I approached a larger group of people— mostly guys– the mean looks stopped and the threatening comments began. I started to feel afraid for the first time that night, like I was in danger. At that point, I was rescued by one of the girls in the group. She told them to leave me alone and offered to help me back to my friend. I gratefully accepted, and my journey continued—this time feeling more confident with someone on my side who looked as if she was very comfortable in a situation like this.

We finally reached Marina, and in perfect timing, because right when we were reunited, Murphy Lee walked out on stage, and the concert began. I thanked the girl for helping me, and Marina and I had a great time the rest of the night, thanks to my anonymous rescuer!

—Liz Niles

Sterling

One day I was going to ride at a stable in Missouri. The stable had just gotten an Akhal Teke. I was very happy to see one because there are only about 50 in the U.S.

His name was Sterling and he was breathtaking! He was named Sterling because, even though he was a buckskin, he shone like metal. He was tall even for a horse, with legs that looked too small to support his large frame. His head was slightly dished or concave. He also had a long neck. He didn't have much mane or tail, but what he did have was ebony. He had dark points, too. (Points are the tops of a horses ears, muzzle, mane and stocking.) The rest of his body was golden brown. If you've seen the movie *Spirit* he looked just like that. He was around 17 hands at the shoulder, a tall horse!

When we came to the fence he looked at us, then at Katherine, his owner. He trotted over to her the long way to avoid us.

Katherine caught him easily and tied him on the pole in the arena area. She put on his saddle pad, then his saddle. She tightened his girth and took off. She led Sterling into the arena and mounted him. She put him into a walk first and it looked as if he was walking on hot coals. He brought his head back and arched his neck. He also brought his knees up so it looked as if he was a high stepper. She brought him to a trot; he stretched his legs, and then went to a canter. He was going so fast he circled the arena in 13 hits.

Then Katherine paced him, which is when the two back feet hit at the same time and then the front legs almost like a mini-jump. It was beautiful!

Katherine brought Sterling in and untacked him. He almost seemed sad that his workout was over. She led him out and he trotted to his stable mate and they started to graze contentedly.

I still think it was an amazing thing to see an Akhal Teke, and I'm still ecstatic that I saw one.

—Brittany Webb

Phantom of the Opera

Once in my young life I thought I just might be in Heaven. I had been on vacation for about a week and a half. My family and I just sailed over to New York from Washington, D.C. My dad (Kevin) had been spoiling our family rotten. We had just seen *Beauty and the Beast* and it was awesome, and now we were at the ticket booth for *Phantom of the Opera.* That was where my heavenly story began.

My dad went into the ticket booth and got our tickets for half price to see *The Phantom of the Opera.* When he came back he said to Brie (my sister), "Look on the chart to see how close we will be to the stage. We are in row BB and seats 100-105." Brie went over to the theater seating chart to see where we were going to go sit. She screamed and I ran over to see why. "We are in the first row!" I couldn't believe it—seeing *Phantom of the Opera* on Broadway and having the best seats in the house! It was amazing.

When we got back to our hotel, the Doubletree, I was so excited I could barely stand it. I was going to be wearing my best outfit that I had brought with me on our vacation, a purple skirt with light purple and blue poke-a-dots and a shirt that went on either side of my shoulders. Its pink, red, white, and light pink stripes went diagonally from left to right. My shoes were ruby red, sort of like

Dorothy's ruby slippers. The shoes were so glossy I could see my face in them.

As we entered the theater I felt like I was walking on the red carpet at the Grammies. We approached the ticket booth and the lady said, "Best seats in the house, enjoy." She smiled and handed our tickets back to us. As we left her my sister leaned down and said, "Carissa, when she said 'best seats in the house,' she meant the best seats in the house!"

When we took our seats I felt like I was the luckiest kid in the world. The theater was enormous. The seats were medium tan brown, with a red violet velvet on the cushion. As I sat down in my seat, number 104, it felt like one of the softest clouds God had ever made.

While my family and I were waiting, I studied the theater. It had a huge chandelier in the middle of the ceiling, and when I looked up at it and then looked at my sister, there were so many spots I could barely see her. The ceiling and the walls were painted off white and the ceiling made an even triangle at the top. The stage was about 10 feet bigger than the Landers Theater's stage. It had amazing artwork sculpted on it like lions and angels, and it was painted gold. The stage was set up in a way that it looked like it was in a dark alley or a home with very dark mysterious lights.

The theater grew dark, and on stage smoke grew and the actors came on. One was standing on something that looked like a mountain or hill. An old man with a coat on half way entered. He had white hair and glasses and was being pushed around by a girl with brown hair. The technical stuff and the backgrounds were amazing. You couldn't hear them when they did all the scene changes. The scenery looked like angels made it, they were that incredible. The costumes were fantastic. I've never seen anything like them. They were like 18th and 17th century clothing for rich people. When you heard actors sing you would just be blown away. They all sang like.... more than words could say! It was phenomenal.

After the show the actors and actresses came out and gave their bows; I stood up because it was great, phenomenal, fantastic! I can't describe how they were. I looked down at my tights and saw that the man who played the phantom was singing with so much feeling and diction that he had spat on my sister and me. I thought it was a little gross, but Brie though it was so cool because she had fallen in love with the phantom! Thankfully, it was raining outside so it would look like I just got some rain on my tights. As we left the theater I knew I would remember this day for the rest of my life.

—Carissa Cassil

My K-Mart Dog

On a blazing hot June afternoon when my mom and I were walking to pick up my brother who was at my cousin's house, my mom decided to make the walk fun. We stopped to get a Sno-Biz at a K-Mart parking lot. There were some people at a bus stop, some people loading their cars, and one little dog wandering around the parking lot. My mom called the dog and it came to us.

There wasn't anyone else calling for the dog so we walked it over to the Sno-Biz to get it some water. After he drank up all the water, we led it over the overpass to my grandma's house. My mom herded it into the backyard, and I got him more water.

The dog was walking back to our house with us when, about 5 houses down from my grandma's house, it darted into someone's backyard and didn't come out. My family went down to our house and put our dog Noble in the garage so he and the other dog wouldn't fight. Then we went looking in the car and found the stray at the same house it disappeared at and asked the man there if he owned him. The man said no, but that he had fed it bread and cat food since he had no dog food. We called the dog over and it jumped in the front seat and rode home with us.

My family put an ad in the paper about a lost dog, and a woman answered it, saying she was the owner's aunt and that the owner didn't miss it. So we kept it after she suggested that was okay. She also said it used to live behind the Quick Trip and that its name was Beau. We kept it and it loves us.

I forgot to mention that it's spoiled rotten!

—Anna Frost

Middled

Some people are in the geek group,
Some people are in the popularity group,
But I'm middled.
Some of my friends are geeks,
Some of my friends are popular.
I just don't know what to do.
Be a geek?
Be popular?
I'm middled.
Geek?
Popular?
Middled?
I'm going to be middled.
That's just right.

—Ashley Ordner

Fear

Fear is something every breathing creation possesses. The word "fearless" shouldn't even be a word at all. Only things that have no emotions or thoughts whatsoever can be fearless. For an ant, fear is humans. For cats, loud noises and things that move too quickly. Everything that God created was created with fear. As for me, I am still scared to this day about one particularly frightening experience.

It was a normal day, a Daylight-Savings day. I went to music lessons, as usual. Sax from 6:00-6:30, and Flute from 6:30-7:00. Palen Music Center was where they were held. The center closed at 7:00 p.m. sharp, but I had no knowledge of this fact.

It was 7:00 when I stepped out of my teacher, Sarah Housewright's, music room. We said our goodbyes and our see-you-next-weeks. I cautiously stepped around the corner of the wall and carefully went down the stairs. The moon was casting its light on the surrounding guitars and pianos.

"See ya, Sweetie," said Jack, the man behind the counter. I carefully pushed the door open, trying not to drop my new saxophone and beloved flute.

I surveyed the parking lot. Nope, no blue Toyota. So I sat and waited. The little outlet mall by Palen was pitch black, as well as the shop itself. I could hear passing cars as I sat my instruments down one by one, and cars slowly left the parking lot.

"What if something were to happen to me?" I thought, "Where will I run if I get approached?" I zipped my jacket up as the night grew colder. I glanced at my watch: 7:05. Okay, only five minutes late. He'll show up. The parking lot still had six cars in it. Some one will save me if I get approached. Someone will, they will...I hope....

A police car had been circling the parking lot for ten

minutes now. It finally stopped in front of me, and a guard rolled his window down to talk to me.

"Your folks coming soon?" he asked.

"Yes, Officer, he should be here in a few minutes!" I answered as calmly as I could. He then drove off. "No!" I screamed inside. "No! I'm all alone, there's only one car left in the parking lot! All of the shops are closed! I'm scared! Come back!"

7:10. The night was even colder, and it seemed ten measly minutes had turned into an hour. Finally, thank the Lord, my friend Jack came up to me and asked me if I wanted to use his phone to call my dad.

I jumped up, politely took the phone, and called my dad. He came at 7:15, with the excuse of, "I didn't know they closed at 7:00 sharp!" Who knew 15 minutes by yourself in the dark could be such horror? The lesson learned: ask the patrol dude to stick around until your ride comes!

—Lauren Smith

Cannes and the French Riviera

There I was, loading a tour bus on my way to France, and leaving the beautiful, amazing, and eccentric lands of Italy behind. As my feet stepped on the bus, I smelled the stale air, which I would have to smell for three or more hours, as long as it would take to reach our first destination in France, the French Riviera. There was a problem though—I had no idea how France would look, smell, or sound! I knew so little about the country, unlike Italy, because I am part Italian, and I knew some of the customs, like Italy's loud voices, parties, great scents, and all types of pasta. I sat there and wondered, "Will France be anything like Italy?"

I sat on the bus, listening to the snoring older people and our guide talking about anything historical over the microphone. All of the noises were starting to drive me insane! I was stuck in this big bus, and I would never be able to leave again! I grabbed my backpack, pulled out my CD player and quickly placed the headphones over my ears. The soothing music of U2 quickly made my mind fly away from the ruckus aboard the metal bus. My eyes slowly started to close, and I dreamt of something I couldn't remember, or perhaps I didn't dream at all.

Quickly I woke up to all of the chatter going on. People were staring out of the windows, whispering to each other loudly, "Look at the scenery! Oh, isn't it beautiful?" Being the curious person I am, I turned my head to look out of the huge windows of our tour bus. They were right; it was beautiful! The sky was almost the perfect turquoise blue, and then below was stunning green grass. Not only that, but the road we were driving on must have been part of a mountain, for when we looked down all we could see was a beautiful river, and what looked like tiny boats, actually huge yachts! It was like a movie or a painting. The beauty of the French Riviera was something you definitely didn't see everyday.

The slope started to lead to a city. It looked like a small city, but after you get up close, you wouldn't even consider it that. The place had large buildings, all beautifully made. The city was clean, with no pollution in sight. From the road, I slowly saw this huge blue blanket crawl over the sand. That was the ocean at the moment the sun was setting, so the blue faded into a sort of purple. It was beautiful, and all I wanted to do was feel the air of the French Riviera, but the stale bus air, starting to smell like body odor, was starting to get to me.

Then our tour guide old us something. She spoke about hotels, and how famous they were. Then she finally said, "We'll be staying in the cheapest hotel in Cannes." That moment I felt this extreme sadness come over me. It was going to most likely be a run-down hotel outside of Cannes, owned by a family. The walls would most likely fall off once you opened the door. Even if I never saw the hotel before, I had a feeling I knew what it would be like. So, I didn't pay attention to the beauty of the city anymore, for I knew it would be ruined once I had to spend the night in the cheapest hotel around.

We continued driving for a little bit longer until something happened. The bus stopped, and out tour guide started giving us instructions about what to do with our belongings. I didn't want to stare out of the window; you couldn't make me. My mother on the other hand was quickly getting her things together and grabbing one of her thousand make-up bags, and instructing me to carry one. I did, since I'm such a wonderful child, (some might disagree). We slowly waited in line to get off of the tour bus.

As I walked outside, I noticed we were still in Cannes. There was a slight relief on me, but then I turned my head and saw this huge hotel. It was a lot bigger than the ones she was talking about. It had peach brick walls and palm trees surrounding it. Huge windows lay along the walls through which you could see big screen TV's. "This is the cheapest hotel in Cannes," my tour guide said. Again she had played another trick on me. I smiled and quickly grabbed my huge red suitcase and started to walk inside. She gave us the keys to our rooms, and I was the first one to reach the elevator. Quickly I stuffed myself inside, but I didn't feel like I was sticking to the walls. This was a big

American size elevator; not to be compared to some other European elevators where you had to sit on top of your suitcase, seriously, just to get to your floor.

When we reached my floor, I walked down the hall to my room. The halls were not damp, like most hotel halls are, and when I used the key to open the door there was a beautiful room ahead of me, and it's something I won't ever forget. The bathroom was huge, and so clean. The walls were the colors of the outside of the building. It had two huge king-sized beds, and a CD player. A nice TV was connected to the wall, and behind the bed was this huge mirror wall. It was so hip and up-to-date. I felt like if this was the cheapest hotel in Cannes, I wondered what the best hotels were like.

Then I quickly had to get ready to go to a tour all over the city of Cannes. We visited tons of places and saw the beautiful dock with all the huge yachts. Then our final place to stop was a casino. I was too young, of course, to go inside the casino, but there was a café where I could sit. I sat there and drank from one of the small cups of coffee, and then I felt a rumble in my stomach. I was slightly hungry, so I went over and bought finger sandwiches. They were the best cold sandwiches I've ever had. They were sweet, but filled with veggies at the same time. I don't know if it was because I was extremely hungry, or if it was really that good. Whatever it was, nothing was better than those sandwiches.

We finished off the day by going back to our hotel, and I went inside to try and fall asleep. I heard the soft roar of traffic, but no honking. Just as I thought I had fallen asleep, I woke up to a wake up call telling me to go outside and explore Cannes before we departed for Lyon. I walked across the beach without a single word coming out of my mouth. The sand never got into my shoes, and the ocean was the deepest blue. It was the best part of the whole time in Cannes. I walked around listening to all the St. Bernards walking around, barking with their deep "woofs," which could only make you laugh.

The time was too soon over, and I now boarded the bus, and smelled again the stale air. This time we were going to Lyon, and I thought that if it was even half of what the French Riviera was, it would be well worth it, no doubt. This was my first experience with France, and since I had a good first impression, even with what Lyon threw at me, it wouldn't change what I thought of the country. France was beautiful. You can't experience what it's like to be in Cannes unless you're there, and once you're there, believe me, you'll never forget it.

—Katherine Mellenbruch

Open-Minded

I remember learning in first grade that everyone is no different from you, and you should treat them no differently. Well, let's face it—we all treat people differently; as much as we wouldn't like to admit it, it's true. But things can change.

Okay, let's move up to sixth grade and my first day at Carver. When you arrive, the first thing you look for are your friends from fifth grade. I remember going to my first class, math, and sitting in the back so I couldn't be called on as much. Then a girl came into the classroom, and I knew some problems would occur.

She was black and had that rugged look to her that would scare you! I thought she was some black kid who lived in the ghetto. I knew what to do: don't look at her, and everything would be fine.

At lunch I saw her again. She looked to be well acquainted with the other black kids. I totally knew this one would be in and out of the office, have bad grades, and have it out with the teachers.

I went to my next class. She was there. This time it was different, though. She sat by me! Very quickly she told me her name and asked me mine. To be nice, I told her. The whole class time we sat and talked. I realized she was going to be one of my friends.

When I started having problems, she was there helping. I soon moved to her table and became friends with the other black kids. I began to realize that everything I thought about her was wrong.

As I always do, I had jumped to conclusions and thought the worst. I was once judged like that, and I thought it wasn't fair, but there I was, doing it to someone else.

For us to understand other people who are different from us, we put them in groups or stereotypes. We may try to tell people it's wrong, but they'll end up doing it anyway. Now being fourteen and in eighth grade, I have learned to be a little more open-minded to other people. Although I may misjudge someone sometimes, I can fix it. Everyone may have trouble with other people, but everything will turn out right if you can just learn to be a little bit more open-minded.

—Jacina Conrad

100 Dollars from the 25-cent Store

On Halloween my brother and I were having fun eating with my mom, Kim, and my grandparents at their house. Our little 3-year-old neighbor, Joshua, came for some candy. His dad drove him to our grandma's house because in the country, neighbors live a little farther away. "Trick or Treat," he said from his little giraffe costume. After a short neighborly visit we waved him "bye" and continued enjoying our family time at the dinner table. About five minutes later another car came up the drive honking its horn impatiently. We were surprised to think we had another trick-or-treater and ran outside to see who it was. Two people were standing at their vehicle shouting, pointing their finger into the air across the valley, "That house, the next house up, is on fire!"

My grandpa yelled, "It's gone, Kim! It's your house, and it's gone!" I looked up the valley where I knew my house had always been securely nestled in the trees and saw yellow-orange flames lighting the night sky. Grandma shouted, "NO!" and ran to the phone and dialed 911, but she couldn't remember the address so Mama took the phone and quickly gave the address. We all hurried to our vehicle and piled in. A lump started to grow in my throat, bigger and bigger, until it made my eyes overflow with tears. I was shaking, but I don't know whether it was from the cold and rain that pelted down on me as I ran to the truck or from the fear rising within me. I didn't have a coat. I left it in my house thinking I wouldn't need it at Grandma's. The truck raced down the gravel road toward the burning home, wheels throwing up rocks and dust into the night air.

It was dark driving down to my house. The only light came from the glow of the roaring flames. When we arrived at the house, we parked in the field, as far away from the flames as possible, to wait for the fire trucks.

It took extra time for the fire trucks to arrive because they couldn't find our house. The fire chief told my mom that our house sits where four fire districts meet, and none of the districts had claimed our spot, so we weren't on any map. The first helpers to arrive were concerned neighbors, but soon the large one-lane gravel road was congested with more people and vehicles than I could comprehend. Some people even parked at Grandma's and walked through the woods. As the night wore on, I saw people risking their lives to save my house, and they didn't even know me. I saw the walls of my house fall as the fire ate them. I saw water spraying from hoses that cut the thick rising bellows of ash and smoke. I thought the burning would never end.

At 1:30 AM, when the embers were dead, the roads cleared, and all the people were gone, I lay through a sleepless night at Grandma's wondering what tomorrow would be like. "Tomorrow" was amazing!!!

People began showing up at Grandma's, where we were staying. . They brought money, clothes and supplies. Many of these people I had never seen before. My friend Sarah went to her church and told what had happened. They gave her $200 to give to us. Sarah also gave some of her own clothes to me. One night a lady came to Grandpa and handed him $180 in cash and said, "consider it a gift from God." The Student Council and teachers from my school took me shopping and I got a brand new wardrobe, or close to one. The most amazing gift came from the heart of a little old lady.

There is a little store in the rural town of Fordland where you pay $0.25 for a piece of clothing. Ruth Caswell, an old lady near 90, lived in the valley where we do when my mom was young. Now that Ruth is old she lives in the town of Fordland, where she manages the "Christian $0.25 store." She heard, as the news of the fire spread through the town, that someone in the valley where she once lived had lost everything. She started calling all the neighbors to see whose house it was that had caught fire. My mom answered the phone when Ruth called Grandpa's house. She explained her quest of finding the house to my mom, and my mom answered, "Ruth, this is Kim and it was my house. We are all fine and unharmed, but we lost everything." Ruth then offered the greatest gift of all. "Kim I am going to send you and your children $100 from my $0.25 store." My mom was overwhelmed, knowing that Ruth would have to sell 400 pieces of clothing to raise that much money. Especially in a small town like Fordland, it could very well take a year to raise that much money. Ruth explained, "The only reason I collect all those quarters is so that someday I can give them to someone in need."

All the money and clothes that were bought and given to my family really helped us out. I never knew people were so generous. I did know there were nice people, but I didn't expect to get so much. After all the kindness given to my family and me, I just wish someday I will be able to return the blessings I received when someone else is in need.

—Jayne Rey

Invisible
In my mind's eye I am everything.
I am a famous movie star, loved by all.
I am a punk rock rocker who never plays by the rules.
I'm all of these things and more in my mind's eye.
But in the eyes of so many others I am but a shadow,
Lost in the vast darkness, invisible to all to all but myself.

—Chelsey Burgess

100% Sure

I didn't live in the safest city in the world. More like the most dangerous city in the world. Every night I heard gun shootings nearby, and the distant train and metro horns. Most people might find all the noises disturbing, but I just barely noticed them. Eventually my house was broken into three times, each time more frightening than the last, but less surprising. My dad then "proposed" that we move to Springfield. I wasn't too sure.

It was a sunny, but cool, in south central L.A. We had been to an exceptionally funny church service. Then we went to the store and bought my brother a board game (1313 Dead End Drive). My dad was fixing the car. Meanwhile, my brother tried to figure out the rules of the game. My brother was lying down on the floor inside the house. My mom and I were leaning against the small white fence in front of our house. We were eating watermelon and talking about the nearby shootings and possibly moving.

Then we heard a very loud, ear splitting, tire screeching! The ensuing sound came from guns of different shapes and sizes. We were about to go inside the house when we actually saw the tire that screeched and the guns of different shapes and sizes.

But in two old beaten cars (one white, the other a dark color) people were shooting at each other from the windows. There was indistinct shouting from the cars. They were probably going at 45-55 mph. My instant reflex was to lie down on the floor so that the shots wouldn't get me. My dad gave me a "get down" signal, but I was one step ahead. The two cars zoomed by firing their guns, leaving the smell of burned rubber and thick smoke. About seven shells landed around me. One single thought kept going through my head, "I'm so dead, that's it, I'm gone, this is, or was, the end for me, and maybe my family is going with me. Now my grave stone can say I died in a shootout!"

I stood back up when I couldn't hear the shots any more, about two minutes. The smell was still there. The smoke they had left behind hadn't taken more than a few seconds to clear away. Some one had called the police. They got there about ten minutes after the event had happened. They picked up all the shells while wearing rubber gloves and put them in a small, clear, plastic bag. The police officers only asked about the people in the cars. All we saw was very dark hands holding the guns.

Fortunately, I lived to tell this story and many others. One thing was for sure though, I was 100% sure I wanted to move out of Los Angeles!

—Jennica Enriquez

What Would We Do Without Her?

My sister Paige, what would we do without her? You see, about four or five years ago, when my sister was in sixth grade, she got sick. Not your everyday cold or flu; she got deadly sick. Well, it started with the flu, but it turned into much, much more. When she got the flu, my parents and I didn't think much of it; everybody gets the flu.

So we kept her home, and when she got better we would send her back to school. One problem—she was not getting better. We started noticing that she was getting thinner and having trouble breathing. We took her to our doctor, who gave us a disappointing diagnosis, "It's just the flu." That couldn't be the truth; it just couldn't!

Well, I guess we were just going to need a second opinion. The second opinion we got turned out to be the same as the first. We knew they were wrong; she was suffering too much just to have the flu!

To be safe, we went back to our doctor a few days later. The truth was told—my sister had pneumonia. It was far past that now though; her right lung had filled with a fluid-like substance. It got even worse; the fluid had turned into gel. The first time we had gone to the doctor, it was still fluid. Then they could have just used a needle to extract it. Now the worst of the worst had happened—Paige's left lung had collapsed like a paper ball. It got covered with a rock-hard substance, and was now rubbing against the heart, causing damage.

It was unbelievable. She was going to need surgery as soon as possible. The surgeons would have to remove the hard substance around the collapsed lung, so after a couple of days her lung would start to expand and become useful. Antibiotics would be used to remove the fluid inside of the right lung.

Paige was in the hospital for ten days, and was out of school for three months. She was miserable in the hospital. Just looking at her made our family feel a pain that was foreign to us; a pain that we probably won't, and don't want to, ever feel again.

If you've ever taken a coffee straw, plugged your nose, stuck it in your mouth, and tried to breathe, it's very hard. Well, that's how she felt all the time. She used all the energy she had to collect air, just so she could stay alive. That's why she got thinner—she ate, but not that often. Plus, most hospital food is gross. She drank water through a straw as often as she possibly could, but had to have it given to her. She didn't have enough energy to even hold up the cup.

I was probably at the hospital from the time school ended to the time I just had to go home and sleep. I did not go to school the day before and after my big sister's surgery. My mom stayed with her every night, and my dad came home with me.

February seventh, the day before my dad's birthday was the day of Paige's surgery. I was a lot younger at the time, so I don't remember everything, and my sis barely remembers a thing. I do remember sitting in the waiting room, waiting for the doctor to come in and tell us whether or not the operator was a success.

As I sat skimming through magazines, my mom was crying, my dad was trying to comfort her, my Grandma Mimi was "reading" the newspaper, and my grandma and grandpa Farrell were talking quietly. We were all worried and scared, and all had the same single thought running through our minds—was Paige going to live? It was the longest night I had ever had, and will probably be the longest I ever have. The doctor finally walked into the room, while all of us were shaking by how nervous we were. When the words came out of his mouth that the operation was a success, I started jumping up and down, literally. My family didn't, but by the smiles of relief on their face and looks in their eyes, you could tell they were jumping inside.

Now in the 2004-'05 school year, Paige is a sixteen-year-old sophomore at Greenwood high school, and is having the time of her life. She goes to a private school, I go to a public one, and we're both having a blast. She is healthy and full of energy. She is smart...well...she makes good grades. Sometimes though, she can be the biggest dork, in a good way, of course. When it comes to the kitchen, um, don't even ask!

My sis is so cool. I can't even imagine what it would be like without her, because she is such a big part of my life. We spend so much time together, when, of course, I'm not with my friends, and she's not with hers. Remember, she is a sixteen year old with a license! My big sis is probably one of the happiest people I know.

From her experience she walked away with three scars, asthma, and bad memories. That's over now, though, and she's having fun and going to live a long, happy, healthy life. My big sis, what would I do without her?

—Ivory Farrell

Camp

I was about six years old when I went on my first camping trip as a Boy Scout. We were camping in a valley, which we later found out to be downhill from a summer camp called Camp Wakonda. It was a beautiful fall day; the air was cool and crisp, with a slight relaxing breeze. I was restless. The result? Time to explore!

Attempting to stay coherent with the "scout way," I followed the buddy system and brought along Jordan. As we roamed the gently rolling hills, our low attention span kicked in—we were bored. Soon Jordan noticed a "mysterious" trail leading uphill through the forest at the edge of the valley. Now, when I say "mysterious," I mean the kindergarten version, a.k.a. "Don't know what it is, so either smash it, question it, tell it you can count to thirty-two, or follow it." We immediately followed.

Trudging up the rocky trail, while thinking what the others would say when we told them we had "boldly gone where no kindergartner has gone before," was pretty easy. At the top of the hill we were acting quite in touch with our "inner explorer" when we heard something rustle in the underbrush. Luckily when we heard its "roar," we became in touch with our "inner one hundred meter dash sprinter."

While running down the trail, screaming at the top of our lungs, "Bigfoot!" and, "Sasquatch! Aaaah!" we kept stumbling over the loose rocks on the trail, eventually twisting our ankles.

We told everyone what had happened, making them all scared, while simultaneously making Jordan and me feel quite pleased with our "brave" selves. We dubbed the path "Sasquatch Alley" when you're walking up, and "Break-Your-Ankle Peak" when you're walking, or running, down. Years later we realized the "Sasquatch" was only the ranger's dog...I think....

—Dalton Robbins

I Feel Secure

When I wake up, I don't have to worry about how I will wash what I'm going to wear, or where I will sleep the next day. I don't have to worry about what, or even if, I will learn, eat, or drink. I have all I need, all I want, and all the love I could ever need. I have a loving family, about eight different wonderful teachers, all the books I could ever read, and a home to live in. I have many different friends, and I have three meals every day.

Other people, however, die every day because of poverty. Some will never go to college because of the knowledge they couldn't buy. Others die from chronic illnesses that we may never find a cure for, such as multiple sclerosis or cancer.

Every day I try to realize how lucky I am. I give all I can, love all I can, and learn all I can through my ever-loving God, and because of this I say I feel secure.

—Tyler Scroggs

Not Another One!

Nooooo, not another one! The day I found out my mom was having yet my third brother, I was soooo mad! Don't get me wrong, I love my brothers, but would it hurt to squeeze another girl in there?

I am in the middle, along with my brother, Eli. I have an older brother, Zach, who turns sixteen in November, a seven year-old brother, Elijah, and a four year-old brother, Dylan. I almost had another brother, but, sadly, it was a miscarriage.

In my house, there is never a moment of silence. I am either fighting with my brothers, or they're fighting amongst themselves. The moment my siblings and I stop fighting, my parents are in an argument! It's never-ending!

Privacy, what privacy? I will love and cherish the day that I can talk on the phone without them on the other phone listening.

You'd think that at least I'd get a break at school, but no, I have to listen to teachers say, "Just ask Zach; I'm sure he remembers doing this." I feel like replying, "I'm sure he does, but why don't you try getting him to help you!"

I suppose that, once in a while, I can love my brothers, like when it's my birthday, Christmas, etc. All I have to say is, every time my brothers annoy me, they can be prepared for "it" when they get older!

It's sometimes hard having brothers and no sisters, because I have nobody to talk to. I know I have my mom, but I don't really like talking about boys with my mom.

Brothers aren't so bad though. Well, I don't want to lie...yeah, they are! But I guess, in some weird way, I am fortunate to have them, all three.

—Brittany Allen

Siblings

They moan, they groan, and they're so annoying! Siblings are your loving, caring brother or sister. Well, not really. They are trained mercenaries out for the hunt, and you're the prey. The parents don't notice; they think they're harmless. That's not the side of them I see.

My brother, Tyler, sure does know how to plan a scheme. He'll kick me under the table and yell, "Ow! Christian, you kicked me!" He also has friends...lots of friends, who all like to get in on the gag. His biggest scheme yet was when he went over to his friend's house to have a Super Bowl party. He then rounded up all of his friends, gave them armor toy guns, and plastic swords, and proceeded to beat on me!

Moving on to my sister, Bailey, who can miraculously fake cry for hours at a time! There are four steps to her tactics: one; she thinks of something to cry about; two, she runs to my mom, bawling and screaming; three, she blames me for something that I would never do, and four, I get grounded. My sister has been known to cry for three hours straight! I know; I timed it!

I do admit that brothers and sisters don't always behave badly. Sometimes, they can even be nice! Most of the time, however, they aren't. That's the problem I have with my siblings.

—Christian Nemmers

Soooo Confusing!

Divorce, popularity, relationships, books, and being in new atmospheres are all problems or good things in our lives; some I'll focus on more than others. But I am going to discuss my feelings, so pay attention.

Divorce is something so hard, especially when you know one parent has left you and your other parent for someone new. Well, that is what happened to me. My dad decided after 17 years that he had not been happy. He found another woman. Well, here is life now: my mom and I live alone. My dad's girlfriend has left. (I don't know which way is left, up, down, or right.) My life is <u>soooo</u> confusing, seriously! My parents say I need counseling, just because I won't talk about my feelings! They talk about me behind my back. How rude is that? So that's my life now and why I am here in Springfield thinking all over again about how to be popular.

Popularity. What can I say about popularity? What is there to say? Through my eyes, everyone is popular. If you think about it, I am right. I am right because popular to me may not be popular to the kids next to me in science. Well, there is one popular "group" that a lot of kids are in—those with divorcing parents. Divorce is sad and unwelcoming. However, it is definitely popular.

Books. Well, this is hard to tie into divorce. If you want to hear something funny—my mom has a divorce book that allows you to not go to attorneys or something to get a divorce. The title is *Divorce Yourself*. I mean who would want to divorce herself? Well, here is some advice: if your parents are divorcing, get a book on it. Trust me, it helps! Relationships can be sooooo confusing!

—Jessica Crowder

My Hero
My hero would be one person that I know very little. As strange as it sounds, it would be my grandma. She is a typical grandma; she bakes the best cakes and always has

the television remote ready. She gives us a ride to and from home and school and never complains, unless she cannot take us to McDonald's afterwards for a cup of ice cream with the cone on top. As I grow older, I find that there are many things that I do not know about my grandma.

I found out first how lonely she was after my uncle Lou stopped living with her. She sent food over every day and called to talk to us. Some days she would even come over and clean. When my grandma's brother, my great uncle moved to town, she made even more food and seemed happier. But, as my mom said, she felt alone without Lon. Her sister died, her parents died, and all she had were my two uncles, my mom, my sisters, and me, besides problematic cousins. I felt powerless, for she had gone through a lifetime of different trends and wars, and I had only lived fourteen years.

One of my most memorable moments with my grandma was my friend Hannah's birthday party. The theme was actresses of the '30s and '40s. I gladly volunteered myself as Audry Hepburn. As I was walking in the garage door from school, it turned out that I was locked out. Thankfully, my grandma had given me a ride and waited for me. We went to her house and waited for my mom to pick me up.

I told my grandma about the party. She walked out of the room and came back five minutes later. She had her old jewelry, which she laid out in front of me. I picked up a diamond bracelet that was hers in high school. She said I could keep it, hoping it would bring me luck. Then she pulled out a tiny purse that had belonged to her grandma. She showed it to me and acted like it was jewelry belonging to the queen herself. She had a smile that I had never seen. She glowed, remembering her days as the flapper, being in the war, and anything else that had happened.

Now, I feel as though every second is precious with my grandma. My jewelry was a success at the party. I know I will never fully understand her, but I can tell Grandma wants to pass her jewelry and traditions down to us. My grandma is my hero.

—Brooke Iler

The Pressures

Sometimes I feel that teachers and parents have no clue what we are going through. They say they do, but how come they do not help us? They seem to make it harder. With everything our bodies are going through, our personal life, and school work, you would think they would help us through it. Even though they have gone through the same things as us, they still do not seem to understand.

Teachers give us a ton of homework, which does not help. They think we can handle it, and some of us can. Others need all the help they can get, because we have more going on. There is a test almost every other day in some classes. I do not have the time for that unless I shut out friends and quit all sports. Even if I did do that, my parents still want me to go do things. By the time I get home from school, eat a snack, and want to rest for 10 minutes, those 10 minutes have turned into two hours gone by. Then I start my homework, which turns into an all night project.

Parents say we need to buckle down and get straight A's, but that is like saying forget your friends, forget sports, heck, why not forget your life. Parents make it hard. With my parents, I am always in trouble. Right now I am having problems getting modules done in technology. They do not understand that you can't work on it at home, and every time I come in, someone else is working on my computer, which means I can't work.

Teachers and parents, both, always say that we have the rest of our lives to be with a boyfriend, but in reality, this leads up to finding your soul mate. I am not going to do anything that I shouldn't with a boy because I do not believe in that, but I can't even hang out with boys as friends! Why can't they trust me?

A teenage life is full of pressures. No matter what type of pressure it is, it is hard. It is so hard. Sometimes I want to rip someone's head off and roll it down the bowling alley, but I know that this time in life will pass. It may not be very soon. It may be in 5 years, but the thought of tomorrow keeps me in today. When will the pressure be off my shoulders? Tomorrow? Next week? Next month? In a year? In five years? I wish someone could tell me.

—Skylar McKee

My Finest Hour

It was a Sunday afternoon. All the boys in my Catholic neighborhood were just getting outside after changing out of their church clothes. The fourth graders were starting up a football game behind the school. My fellow third grader, and good buddy, Joey, was a short and husky kid. He wasn't really big, but he wasn't scrawny like I was. I was a short and skinny kid. But I had big friends.

As we strolled along, the fourth graders asked if one of us could play. Joey had dinner to go to, so I played. Looking back on it all, I think the fourth graders just wanted a little kid to pound upon. Being the giddy little boy I was, I just wanted to play and that I did. I did that very well.

I didn't only contend with these boys, I was the star of the game! I took every hit. I felt invincible. I ran the ball up the middle, "Bam!" tackled by the biggest kid in the fourth grade. I didn't feel a thing. I got right back up. They couldn't catch me! I was dodging tackles left and right, making touchdown catches, diving plays, and one-handed grabs. I was doing it all. And when they couldn't catch me, they hit me hard.

Some kids were getting so frustrated with my game. I remembered a guy named Tim; he just couldn't tackle me. He was so ticked. The next time I got by him, he started saying some harsh words. He charged. I charged. Everyone tried to hold us back. He continued his cursing at an extreme volume. I cursed back while both of our teams were restraining us. I got a free hand and threw a punch. I missed entirely. He was too far away and the mob holding me was powerful.

They let us go when we calmed down, and I walked home. My hour was over, as was the game. I crowned myself MVP, and that was the last of it. It was my finest hour.

—Robert Schaeffer

Of Love and Hate

It is in the hearts of men that love and hate reside,
Both are vastly strong and neither will subside.
Love consists of passion; hate consists of pride.

However,
There is a single truth in which one can confide:
There is no single point in time at which they coincide.

To love is to adore, to feel blissful deep inside.

To hate is to abhor, and truly to despise.
The temperaments of both are not the least bit pacified,
For half the time when called upon,
One really can't decide.
Between affection and aversion,
There is a great divide.

And throughout all of this confusion,
One conclusion is applied:
There is no single point in time at which they concide.
                                                —Christian Cook

The Party
    There she was
In the middle of a sea of people
With a face of a scared little girl
        Orange on black
        Bordeaux on white
Looking frightened and alone
        Our eyes connect
        Emerald on violet
        Violet on emerald
She rushes into my arms
Trembling with anxiety
        And I hold her
The duration of the party is spent
The two of us sitting on the couch
            Together
        Her hand in mine
        My hand in hers
Head on my shoulder
        Orange on black

Bordeaux on white
Pale, pale white
Resting on my shoulder.

—Brittany John

War Times
Cities fall.
Heroes rise.
One person lives, another dies.
A tank rolls on, a helicopter flies.

"Get the terrorists!" they say.
That's why soldiers wake up everyday.
There's one reason they fight.
One reason they push on day and night.
It's the hope of a white dove's flight.

But hope is far from real.
We live in a world where people kill and steal.
Nothing seems to have changed.
Our world seems even more estranged.
Cities fall.
Heroes rise.
One person lives, another dies.
A tank rolls on, a helicopter flies.

—Austin Lamb

The Chinese New Year
You know what's really weird? That every culture has
different holidays and different ways they celebrate them.
In China, the Chinese New Year is the most important

holiday of them all. I remember one in particular; it was last year's Chinese New Year.

"Mom! Pour in the crab!" I yelled at my mom over the boiling pot. She gave me a look before pouring in some more water. This may seem strange for you guys, but it was a regular Chinese New Year for me. As my mom put in more of the food, my sister and I argued over who got what. There are usually crabs, noodles, vegetables, dumplings, and lots of seafood. We usually all sit around a big table and just talk.

"So how much do you think we'll get this year?" This was a frequent question my sister would ask me every year.

"I don't know, not much." My usual answer.

"Probably."

After asking the question each year my sister and I would dig into the yumminess on the table. Then, finally, when we were all done eating (well at least half way), my mom and others would pass people a small, red envelope. My sister and I were usually the last ones.

"Here you go" my mom said as she handed me the envelope. I could feel the texture of what was inside, as my sister and I greedily tore our envelopes apart. Then my sister stared at hers, a little dumbfounded.

"Fifty dollars? Are you serious? This is it?"" Normally there would be a little over a hundred. I looked at my mom before saying, "What is going on mom? She gets fifty while I get thirty?" Mom glared at me. "She's older, besides, this is only from me. I'll give you what your relatives send later."

My sister eye-balled me as if to say "you know she's going to keep it right?" I just shrugged and went back to my food.

The Chinese New Year might not seem like a big thing

in America, but for my family, you can say it's pretty huge. It's the time for bad deeds to be forgotten, setting new goals, and of course, a new age. It may seem weird but the Chinese have two birthdays. One's on their actual birthday and one is on the Chinese New Year, when they 'grow' a year. You can say its a pretty big thing in China, so big they close school for one month for it (of course summer break is only two months.)

Every year, one month before the Chinese New Year, my mom would put all sorts of decorations up. Everything is usually red. We have the Chinese 'gold', the word 'luck' turned upside down for even better luck, and of course, whatever animal of the Chinese zodiac it is that year. (This year is the dog.) It's a very important time of the year for our family; I have been celebrating it for just about all of my life. And to think, we did all that just to celebrate an upcoming new year.

"Wendy! Turn off the lights!" my mom yelled at me. I looked at the clock. 2:00 A.M. it would usually say. I sighed, thinking about where I'd hidden my stash, about what happened last year, about what kind of things will happen next year. Then I tip-toed out, and watched the first sun-rise of the Chinese New Year, just like I did on New Years Eve.

—Wendy Zhang

Guadalajara, Mexico

In your neighborhood, what's it like? Is it a nice suburb, is it busy and bustling, or does it make you want to look around every corner for fear of somebody mugging you? Have you ever felt like moving somewhere else? I have and I did move—so I'm going to tell you about

Guadalajara Mexico.

When I moved there I couldn't read or write in Spanish so I didn't know what all the signs meant. Over there, all the stop signs said "alto" which I later learned read "stop." I lived in a three story house with my grandma. Outside of my house there were always kids playing soccer or football. In Spanish football means soccer and you have to say American football to mean the football you play in the U.S. Anyway, you can just walk out there and somebody would put you on the team. What I mean is that instead of trying to gain the courage to ask if you can play you just have to walk outside!

One thing I can remember most about Mexico is the food! You can have rice, tacos, and enchiladas, all in the comfort of your own home! The corn on the cob is so good over there. The corn is white and isn't sweet but when you put lime juice, salt and peppers on it, it's like the best food ever!

I have never liked school but school in Mexico was so incredibly different that it was fun! The hard part was that I didn't know how to read or write in Spanish so I had to learn over the summer! Once I could read though, school was pretty easy except for math. In fouth grade we were already doing long division! During recess, we would play all kinds of games. When we could get a hold of a ball, we would play soccer. If not we would then play games like tag or freeze tag. There was one game where you would split the people that played into two groups. Then, one group would have to be it while the group had to hide. If they caught you, you would go to the "prison" zone that you would choose beforehand. You could rely on your teammates to pull you out without getting caught or you could try to get past the kids guarding you. The cool thing is that you could catch people forcibly, guard people forcibly, you could basically do everything forcibly!

All in all, I liked going to Mexico because it was different than what I am used to here in the U.S. All the things I've seen and experiences I've had have made a big impact on my life. That's why I like to travel; I love always having fun and learning too!

—Arandi Lopez

A.N.Z.A.C. Day

A.N.Z.A.C. Day is a national commemoration for Australia and New Zealand. It stands for : Australian and New Zealand Army Corps and it is celebrated on April 25th each year. Even though I am Chinese, I grew up in Tazmania (the island under Australia), and I still celebrate it.

At school we'd always make paper poppies; it is the flower used to celebrate A.N.Z.A.C. Day. All day we would do worksheets in our classes about the war , and one year we learned about "the unknown soldier." During some point of the day we would take a minute or two of silence.

My favorite part of the day was going home and stuffing my stomach with "anzac" cookies. They are cookies that taste like sugary carmel with oats in them.

A.N.Z.A.C. Day is actually similar to Memorial Day in the United States. It is a time to remember all the soldiers who died for a country. Now that I am in the U.S. I often think about that special day—especially on April 25th!

—Cindy Quan

Kenya

"Habari yako"—that is Swahili for "how are you." Going by the language, you would think I am from Tanzania, but no, I am from a beautiful country called Kenya. What makes it so beautiful you may ask? The wildlife, the jungles, and the people with their different cultures.

In Kenya, there are three major ethnic groups. They are the Bantu, the Nilotes and the Cushites. These groups have hundreds of tribes in each of them and they are completely different from each other. I can't begin to go over all of the information about each tribe, but I can describe my own.

My tribe is called the Kikuyu tribe. It's the largest tribe in Kenya, making up 21% of the population. A popular story is told about how the Kikuyu tribe was made. It started when God told Gikuyu and his wife Mumbi to build their home at the top of Mt. Kirinyaga (Mt. Kenya). Over time they had nine daughters named Acera, Agachiku, Aairimu, Ambui, Angare, Anjiri, Angui, Aithaga and Aitharandu. The names are hard to pronounce, but not for me. Each of the daughters represents a Kikuyu clan and have become the names of women in the Kikuyu tribe, but with "w" at the beginning of the names.

The Kikuyu people are agricultural—they live on farms. They plant all kinds of food: mandizi (banana), bebe (corn), kahawa (coffee), sukuma wiki (kale) and nyanya (tomatoes). They also take care of herds of cattle.

I know some things about my tribe, but I especially remember my own life there as a young boy. Back in Kenya, we played a lot of soccer every day. We called it football and it is the country's most popular game. My friend and I played it a lot, and we also tried something new, a game called "cricket." That is a game not much different from baseball, but the bat is wider and the ball is stronger. We also played rugby.

Sometimes I miss the beautiful country I will always

call my home. I love to think about all of the things that make the culture special.

                              —Charles Kagogo

Still Life—Brittany John
Carver Middle School

Stain Glass—Kori Chrismer

Dreams—Brandon Cole

STUDY
MIDDLE
SCHOOL

The Boy Break Up

He's joking, he's just joking, I thought to myself as my boyfriend told me the worst news I heard that night. He's just telling me this to get back at me for locking him in the shed, I thought, but something deep in me told me this was no prank. I didn't even think when I said it. It sounded so stupid when it came out, but all I could mutter was, "Are you serious?" His answer wasn't too great either. "Yes," was all he said. Yes, yes, yes, that word echoed through my mind until I came up with another stupid question, "Why?" Again he answered a bad answer. "There's someone else," he replied. Those words hit me like super sharp needles, and pain broke out all through my body. Once more I came up with another stupid question that I already knew the answer to. "So you've been cheating on me?" "Yeah," was all he said. I could feel fury rising, but I kept it inside. I wouldn't be able to restrain much longer. Soon the beast from within would emerge.

As I stood glaring into those dark brown eyes that I

thought I could trust, I realized I couldn't be that mad at him because I had cheated too. My expression softened slightly when I said, "Umm, I've been seeing someone else, too." I couldn't' believe what he said after those regretful words. He furiously said, "What, I'll kick his butt!" Now like a volcano suddenly coming out of a dormant stage, I exploded, "I can't believe you!" I yelled. "I didn't say I was going to kick your girlfriend's butt, did I?" "Well, no you..." he started. "You disgust me," I interrupted. I whipped around and took a breath of the night air. A small squirrel darted across the road as it started to rain.

When I finally turned around to talk to him, he was not there. I dropped my shoulders sadly and started to walk home. "Wait!" someone called out. I turned around again to see my official ex-boyfriend. "I thought my first break-up would end with a...well...errrr.....a goodbye kiss," he said. "In your dreams boyfr..." I started but then I said, "In your dreams ex-boyfriend." I turned around once more and walked home, leaving him in a complete shock.*

*I regret to say I have not seen Joey since I said those last words to him.

—Brittany Hurt

Winter Night

Winter night,
Starry night.
Cold, chilling,
Dark is the atmosphere.
But I am here,
On a never-ending trail.
In the woods I see

A small house,
Warm, cozy.
But I will never stop
Until I find
My destiny.

—Regan Fink

Gone

Boom! I heard the car door shut as I stood there taking my last look at them, knowing there was a good chance I'd never see them again. Kimberly just two years old and Katie, four almost five. What would happen to them? They had lived with us for a year and two months, but even at that we were family. They were my cousins. I couldn't let them go. I had been annoyed and argued with them and even said some things I regret saying, but I still loved them. Deep down I wanted them to stay.

Seeing the tears run down Katie's little checks and Kimberly looking around wondering what was happening, I fell apart inside. My heart was melting. I broke down in tears and fell to my knees in the driveway. I covered my face and then took one last look at them as they drove away. Even with the windows up I could hear Katie screaming.

I went inside and buried my face in my bed and screamed as loud as I could as tears streamed down my face. Would I ever see them again? Would they remember us? Would they hate us when they got older for giving them up, or would they be happy because we did the right thing? All these questions were flying through my head.

I looked up and saw my empty room. No toys, no toddler bed, no Katie, no Kimberly. I went outside and ran to get away. As I ran I got tired and started walking around the block.

I could just remember those little arms around my neck holding me tight, and little Katie saying, "Sissy, don't let me go."

It was too late; I had already let go. I hadn't let go of them in my heart, but they were still gone.

This was a lesson learned for me. You should always follow your heart. If it says let go, do it. If it says hold on, do it. In my mind I wanted to let them go, but in my heart I wanted them to stay. I look back on that cool fall day and wish I could relive it and bring them back. I didn't listen to my heart. You can't relive the past, so make the right decision the first time.

Katie is now six and Kimberly is three. We haven't seen them since. But who knows what the future holds? Maybe they'll come back? Remember, listen to your heart; your head can be stubborn!

—Racheal Hawthorne

My Experience with Diabetes

Ever since life began, there have been diseases. I can tell you about a certain one, diabetes. It's a horrible thing to have. You see, there is a thing in your body, insulin, and when you have diabetes, your body stops producing it.

Insulin is something your body uses to break down sugar so it doesn't get too much of it. Insulin is so important, that without it your body would have too much sugar, and you would go into a coma. Actually, insulin is really cool; it's like it controls your whole body. Without insulin your body would start to act up. It would start to eat your muscles for nutrition, and you would get weaker and weaker. Diabetes is a horrible thing to go through. If you ask me how I know, I'll tell you how—from personal experience.

The experience began in December. I was excited about Christmas because this year I got to go with my real dad for Christmas. The first few weeks went by really fast. I went sledding, hung out with my friends at the mall, skating rink, etc. Finally, it was Christmas week. One day, two days, three days went by so fast. The next thing I knew, it was Christmas Eve. That night I spent the night with my mom, dad, Toni, and Jacob, opening presents, laughing, just having a good time.

The next day my real dad came to pick me up around five o'clock and I spent Christmas with him and his girl-friend in Lexington, Missouri. My dad got me a C.D. player. It was so cool. I listened to it all day when we were in the car going to my uncle's, aunt's, grandpa's, and grandma's to open presents.

A few days later I started to sleep all the time, and was becoming a real grump. My dad asked me if I was okay. I said I was just fine, but tired from all the school activities I'd been doing. Finally, the long sleepy week at my dad's was over and he took me back home.

The next day I had school. It was so easy that day at school. All we did was sit back and learn people's names. It was around mid-January when I started to fall asleep every single day in class. My teacher kept getting on to me and sending me to the nurse's office. One day the nurse took me into her office and weighed me; I was 95.5 pounds. That was okay with me, because most of the time I weighed 119.5 pounds. The nurse called my dad and he got concerned and called the doctor for an appointment the next day, my birthday.

The next day my mom took me to the doctor. He examined me, checked my throat and took x-rays to make sure my bones were okay. When she weighed me, I weighed 88.5 pounds. Overnight! My doctor was concerned about me. She started questioning me, "Are you doing drugs? Are you smoking?" All of those questions were, of course, a BIG "NO!"

An hour later the test results came in. Then the nurse said that I had Type 1 diabetes. By that time I had burst into tears. I was thinking to myself, "Will I be the outcast of the school?" and "What will my friends think of me having diabetes?" After awhile my dad came in, so my mom broke the news to him. Then the doctor came in and said they were doing everything they could to get me to a diabetic specialist. The bad thing was that day was my b-day and we had the whole thing planned. First, we were going to eat Chinese food for lunch, then for dinner we were going to go to Incredible Pizza. After all that we were going to go to the Battlefield Mall to go shopping for clothes, and then to get my ears pierced, twice. Instead we got the directions to the Columbia hospital.

It was a long, long drive. When we finally got to Columbia, we got lost and had to ask for directions, TWICE. Then finally we made it to the hospital. I went to the children's section, and my mom went to check me in to see the doctor. It was late when my mom got done checking us in at the desk. The doctor finally said, "Nora Key, let us show you to your room." So they took us to the second area that was the kid's section.

The hallways were full of color and different pictures of trains, like farm animals and a farmer tending his chickens. There were lots of other paintings, too, but my favorite of them all was the one across from my room. It was a painting of a train, and every time I went by it there was a light in the front that went on. The train had lots of color and decorations on it. When they showed me my room, it was so cool.

My room had little TV's that I could pull down from the ceiling and watch all sorts of things on them. Also there was a TV that my family and I could watch together. They also had chairs and a couch.

After I had admired my room, I put on my p.j.'s. Then the nurse walked in with a needle in her hand. When I saw it, I started to get really nervous. My heart started to beat really, really fast, like a wild grizzly bear was chasing me. I thought to myself, "Oh great, this is going to hurt!" I hate shots. She said, "Turn over." Then she gave me the shot right in the bottom!

About 10 or 20 minutes later, the nurse came in again and said, "Time for your IV." Then she said, "Do you want someone to go with you?" I turned and looked at all the family that was there for me and said, "I want my dad to come with me to the IV room." The nurse gave me a book to read to get the pain off my mind. When they started I couldn't feel anything until they kept poking me and poking me with the IV. The nurse said that I had "rolling veins" and that they would have to stick the IV in my wrist. I knew right then and there that I had "rolling veins" because of my Grandma Tammy!

I didn't go back to the same room. They moved me into the room right next to the train. I was so happy because it had my favorite painting right next to it. When I lay in that new bed, it was even more comfortable than my last one. But after awhile the bed started not to be as comfortable as I thought it was. It felt like a thousand pointy little needles were going in my back.

The next week in Columbia was a nightmare. It was the most boring week ever. All there was to do was to watch TV. When you watch TV over and over again, all you see are reruns. I think the only interesting part was meeting my diabetic specialist team. They gave me lots of interesting things to do and have fun with. They also taught me how to take care of my diabetes. After a whole week in the hospital, they finally let us go home. I was so excited to go home to see all my friends and sleep in my own bed. The day I went home was the best day of the whole entire week.

I think no kid should get diabetes. It has to have a lot of attention. You have to have shots or pills depending on what type of diabetes. If you have Type 1 diabetes, you have to take shots. You can't take pills, because it's not enough for your body to break down sugar. If you have Type II diabetes you can take pills or shots; it just depends on what our body does. You also have something called a meal plan to follow, but it's not a diet. It's when you limit your amount of food to keep your sugars under control. Diabetics have to pay attention to the carbohydrates they eat or their sugars will get too high and that's bad. Figuring the numbers builds good math skills! So that is the story about my disease and how I handle it, but from this day on, I will still hate having diabetes.

—Nora Key

My Biggest Flashback

It's spooky. One Saturday night, my cousin came to stay with me. Before we went to bed, we started to talk about our Uncle Milo. All of a sudden we saw him flying around us. He was a beautiful angel. About two or three years before, Milo had died.

Just after that I started seeing all of the people in my family that had died. The first person I saw was my grandpa Russell. Then after that I saw my grandpa Earner. I also saw Milo again. The last person I saw was my step-grandpa Brown.

Sometimes I have flashbacks of their looks. Sometimes I have flashbacks on things like what we did together. In fact as I write about it, I'm having a flashback. I say to myself, "How do I know this is Grandpa Russell? I don't even know him. Ashley, my 15-year-old sister, didn't even know him. How do I know all of this about someone I don't even know?"

Nobody will ever understand how scared we were and how we still feel about the horrible flashbacks that hurt us even to think about. But I still have questions. Why is this happening to us? Is it a sickness? Why are these people coming back? Are they trying to tell us something in particular?

—Lacey Arner

The Kingdom
You have heard the tales
Of where I spent my childhood.
It was a restless place
Of no sleep
And never-ending shouts
And screams.
It was once a kingdom of happiness.
But now
All my memories
Of good times in that place are lost.
—Kevin Robb

Kathy's Stroke

Bang! Kathy hit the floor. She screamed as she collapsed down. Whoosh! My dad flew past me to find out
what had happened. She had had a stroke! That morning
we were all getting ready. She had started some breakfast
while she was fixing her hair and putting on makeup.
Then out of the blue, she just fell to the floor. As I saw her
hit the floor, my dad ran back there trying to lift her up,
but how? The doctor later said her whole right side of her
body was dead; it went into shock. I was in shock, too.

As I saw Kathy on the floor, half of me wanted to go to
her, but the other just told me to stay put. I thought for a
minute then decided to go. While I was walking toward
her, I heard my dad screaming at my Uncle David to drive
down to Bill's to call an ambulance. All of a sudden, I
couldn't move. My other Uncle Robert was holding me
back from going to Kathy. I started to scream and cry,
panicking all at once. I couldn't think. I had just woken
up. My crying, screaming, and all the sounds around me
all at once were hard to understand. They were all just one
BIG blah!

One month later I could finally go see her. As soon as
I walked into her hospital room, I sensed wonder. She
didn't look anything like my step-mom. Her whole head
was swollen. Doctors had cut her beautiful bangs back so
far to do surgery, you could see all of her forehead.

There was a long line of thirty stitches. She had lost
more that fifty-percent of her brain. Dad told me as we
walked in the hospital room she might call me a different
name. As I walked towards her bed she said, "Brian? Is that
you?" It seemed as if she was blind, but she wasn't. So I
said, "No, Mama, it's Destiny, your step-daughter." She
said, "Ooowh...come here." So I did, and you know what?

She remembered me. She gave me a big hug and she whispered in my ear, "I love you!" I said, "I love you, too!"

After that I went back to grandma's house and waited for another month or so for Kathy to get out of the hospital.

Even now, years later, I still remember everything about Kathy's stroke. So I learned not to worry as much and you never should either, because you never know how something will turn out!

—Destiny Kidd

Breaking Arms

Once when I was in third grade, I was playing in my friend's yard with my friend Katie, and my older sister, Victoria. Katie was about five feet tall. She had nice brown hair and lime green eyes. Victoria was was a little shorter, with lovely brunette hair and forest green eyes.

We were trying to do cartwheels and we were doing a pretty good job. Victoria and I were doing just plain simple cartwheels. But suddenly Katie said, "That's not how you do a cartwheel. You have to run, jump, then do it." So she went and did it, but what she didn't tell me to do was jump after you land, then do the cartwheel. So I went. I ran and then I jumped and started doing the cartwheel in the air. When my arm hit the ground it had all my weight and the impact of the jump on it. Suddenly, everything went black! When I woke up a few seconds later, I felt like I was about to hurl. I felt a sharp pain in my arm and when I looked down I lightly shook my arm and it looked a bit like Jell-O. Victoria and Katie were hovering next to me.

Katie helped me up. Then Victoria helped me across the street to our house. When I got home, I was ready to cry, my arm hurt so much. I slipped off my shoes and I noticed my mom working in the kitchen. Then I saw my dad on the computer. I hurried over to him so he could check on my arm. My mom asked, "What's wrong, honey?"

My dad replied, "I think Jackie broke her arm. I'll call the hospital to warn them we're coming." While my dad tried to call the hospital, I sat on the couch and tried to eat some macaroni and cheese, but my arm hurt too much.

About two hours later (though it felt like a million) my dad took me to the hospital. It took so long because my dad had to keep holding for them a long time and he also had to find my file. When we got to the hospital I got my arm x-rayed. The x-ray room looked like the lab of a mad scientist. It was dark. Huge tubes ran across the ceiling and a big machine roared in the back with flashing buttons and lights. I rested my arm on the table in the middle of the room while the doctor fiddled with the machine in the back. Then a tube made of steel came down with a light at the tip of it and went back and forth across my arm. It was scary!

It turned out I broke the bone in the middle of my arm, fractured it about an inch from my elbow, and fractured it on my elbow. The doctor also told us that about eight other girls had broken one of their bones that night as well. He said since I had popped it out of place, I would have to have surgery on it.

Two weeks later, I couldn't eat for almost a whole day because I had to have surgery, so I was really crabby. In between then I had to stay home from school, so mostly I watched movies. It was hard to do a lot of things, but I got over it. Anyway, I had the surgery late at night, and I still had to have the sleeping medicine even though I was out cold! And the nurse promised me a Popsicle after it was all over, but I never got one!

After the surgery, my mom told the doctor to give me a purple cast. They did! I thought it looked cool, but we did need to get gel markers so people could sign it. My mom and I had to go home in a taxi that night because our van broke down. My dad got a ride with the tow truck.

I had to wear the cast for six weeks. It kept me from doing a lot of things. It was hard to brush my teeth, get dressed, and other stuff like that, but unfortunately it didn't keep me from going to school!

—Jackie Bradley

Hank Aaron

755. What is so important about that number? Well, to most people who know anything about baseball, it means a lot. But what is so important about it? Well, it's the record for career home runs in baseball. Who set the record? It was set by Hank Aaron.

Henry Louis Aaron was born on February 5, 1934, in Mobile, Alabama. He started playing semi-pro baseball at just age 15, for the Mobile Black Bears. When he graduated from high school, he played with the Indianapolis Clowns. He drew the attention of many agents. One of them was from the Milwaukee (now Atlanta) Braves. Eventually, he signed with the Braves and started playing for their minor league teams. Hank was on his way.

He didn't stay in the minors very long, though. He was only there for two seasons (1952-1953) when he started playing in the Major Leagues. He was booed and jeered by the crowds when he started playing in 1954. The white fans didn't like a black person playing on the team.

Despite that fact, he still didn't give up. In fact, he won batting titles in 1956. But that wasn't the best he was going to do.

In 1957, Hank Aaron not only won MVP, but he helped the Braves win the World Series that year. By the time he retired, he'd hit 755 total home runs, (a record) 2,297 RBIs, 6,856 total base hits, and 1,477 extra base hits. He had been at bat 12,364 times in his career! For a while, after he retired, Hank worked as the now Atlanta Braves' director of player development. In 1982, he was inducted into the National Baseball Hall of Fame. Now, at 71 years old (72 in February), he is the Vice President of player operations for the Atlanta Braves.

The reason I admire Hank Aaron is because he faced so much opposition when he started baseball, but didn't give up. In fact, he set the career home run record! He also helped the Braves win the World Series and MVP in the same year. Hank stuck in there and didn't give up.

—Colin Wilson

Life Told How It Is

Life is something given to all of us. We have our ups and downs. We have our friends and foes. We can be brave or we can be afraid. When you are born, you were alive, but you had not truly lived, yet. Days passed to weeks, weeks to months, and months to years. You learned something small but very important: you learned how to crawl, how to walk and talk a little. Though small, it was important that you learned how to get around.

Now you are six. You know how to walk, talk, maybe even read and write. You've started kindergarten. You have done may important things in your life, many of them small. You have hopefully made a lot of friends. You might be learning the lesson that you don't always get your way. You're old enough to take on some chores now, like cleaning your room, and helping your mom with the dishes.

You're now eleven, and in sixth grade. You have done a whole eleven years of living. Each and every day of those years you have done something important. You've learned how to read, write, add, subtract, multiply, and divide. You have learned to say no to drugs, and what to do in case of an emergency. Most of the things you will use everyday of your, hopefully, long life.

You have finally hit sweet 16. You're tired of your mom treating you like a little kid. You're attracted to those of the opposite sex. You've had your first out of family relationship, or in other words, you've had your first girlfriend or boyfriend. You're acting like any normal teenager would; you stay out of the house as much as you can, hang out with friends more than family; yeah, that kind of stuff. You have done more important things in your life, some more important than others. The less important stuff is like going to your first dance and your first date The more important stuff is like, not only do you know how to say no to drugs but also to things that make you have a bad feeling like sexual things or cheating on a test. You're ready to choose the road you want to go on, victory or loss. It is your life. It's your choice.

You are now an adult. If you chose the road of loss, you are either in jail or on the run from the law. If you chose the road to victory, you most likely have a good paying job and a family. Even if you don't have a job, but you have a loving family (it doesn't even matter if you're a 'punk loving' family) you have still chosen the road to victory. Those of you who chose the road to loss, maybe you can start a new life. It's never too late.

You are now a senior citizen and you have retired from your job. Your kids have grown up and your life has paid off. You might need a little help in your life now. Maybe with getting around or even eating. You know your family still loves you no matter how old you get, but you wonder if they will come and visit. You have lived your life and you are ready to let go. The only thing stopping you is that your family is not ready to let go of you. You hold on as long as you can until finally you have to pass on.

Life as we know it changes everyday. You have friends, foes, fears, bravery, but most importantly you have yourself. You don't have to do what others tell you, just be you. It is your life. It is your choice.

—Brittany Hurt

Friends

Friends are the most important thing to me. Without friends, you pretty much have nothing. Some good qualities that a good friend might have are: they're nice, they're not afraid to talk to you about stuff, they're always there for you, and they're funny. They make you laugh when you're sad or feeling down.

I don't know what I would do without my friends! What I mean is we couldn't hang out, stay the night at their house, or they could come over to mine. Friends are really important, but if you treat them unfairly, you will never have any. Then when you sit by yourself in the cafeteria you probably would be made fun of. And that's not fun. When I walk around with my friends, I see people getting made fun of, and that's definitely not funny.

When you don't have friends to help protect you, sometimes you might get picked on. A lot of people think it's funny to make kids cry that are smaller and younger then they are. They think they're cool when they walk up to little kids, back them up against something and get anything they want. But if a little kid keeps on giving in, he will keep getting picked on. Sometimes it takes the bully being picked on by a bigger kid before he will stop picking on the little kids. Then they will know how it feels to be bullied.

If you don't have any friends you will have everything stuck inside you. You can't get it out unless you talk to someone, and that's what friends are for. Friends are always there for you. If you were getting beaten up, they would help you.

See, if you don't have friends, you pretty much have nothing. As everybody says, treat people how you want to be treated. It's true. When I treat my friends with respect, I get respect right back. So just treat everybody with respect.

Friends really are the most important thing to me. Remember it's important that people really shouldn't pick on or beat up other people. If you want friends, you've first got to be nice. Then get to know each other and perhaps you'll be best friends forever.

—Andrew Choate

My Dad

My dad is very cool. He loves to do a lot of fun stuff like go skating, swimming, and a whole lot of other stuff. But right now, he is building a house down in Kimberling

City, so that his girlfriend Tammy, her daughter Devin, and my wonderful dad can move down there right away.

I know that every other weekend I go down there I will like it, because in the spring and summer I will get to go swimming. In the fall and winter I'll burn leaves and trash, and stay very warm. The good thing about that is I'll be with my wonderful dad.

My dad used to have a clubhouse when he was little, and he showed it to us. Now we have our own clubhouse by the water. It is really beautiful there.

One more thing, I can't wait until my dad gets it done, because he will be happy, and when my dad's happy, everybody's happy. The only thing I don't like is sitting in the car for an hour and a half to see him, but it isn't that bad.

I'm a little upset that he is moving because I have to give up my room, and I won't get my own room. I love my dad no matter what. He also said when we get the house finished we might be able to get a dog, and I was very happy about that.

I can't wait until I get to spend the whole weekend with just my dad, my brother, and me. I love my dad very much, and I know he loves me, too. I wish my mom and dad could get back together one of these days, and we could live happily ever after.

—Amanda Powers

Brittany, Accident Princess!

Brittany has been through so much in her young life. When she was a baby, she almost died because of a bad heart valve. She was on a heart monitor, and had to go to the doctor every day to get a shot. Every other day, she had to go just for a check up. Now, she only has to go if she is sick.

When she was four, she cut the tip of her finger off, but the nurse said she would probably have to finish taking it off. Then the practitioner came in and said she could sew it back on, but she most likely would not have a fingernail. Guess what? The nail actually did grow back!

When Brittany was six, she broke her arm. Her bone broke in two spots, but she didn't cry until Mom told her she couldn't fix it. Another time Brittany and Trisha were jumping rope on the trampoline, and Brittany flew off. What happened? I picked her up and ran to the house. Brittany and I were both screaming. I put her on the chair. That was another trip to the emergency room. Guess what they told her? She broke her collarbone, but she was fine.

Then Brittany and I were jumping in a trampoline another time, and she flew in the air. She landed on her face. She ran to the front yard where my mom was standing. Mom said she would be fine and sent her to get some ice.

About a month ago, Brittany was riding her bike. Mom went inside to check on the brownies she had in the oven. I went outside because she was riding through ditches. She flipped onto the road face first. Brittany ran to the house screaming, "I'm bleeding! I'm going to die, Mommy!" My big sister Ashley went to pick up the bike and found blood on the road from Brittany's face. Her face was still bleeding and she didn't remember anything. Mom took her to the hospital. They said she had a concussion and could possibly have a tumor or a cyst in her brain.

It turns out she does have a cyst in the main part of her brain. My mom showed me the MRI on a disc. Parts were a little scary. Brittany may possibly have little cysts all over her brain. The main cyst is in the main part of her brain. The MRI disc showed her skull and more interesting things. One of them was her eye. When my mom put it on the computer to look at the MRI pictures, the doctor told her that all of the white spots might be little cysts.

When Brittany had her MRI, lots of people took off of work to see how it went. The doctors put her to sleep. Then they put the stickers on her chest to keep up the heart-rate, and they put her in a big circular tube. She said that from what she remembers it was scary.

It's been a few months now, but Brittany is doing great, even if she forgets things sometimes. Well Brittany is still her ordinary, young self—the accident princess!

—Lacey Arner

That Boy
The boy I dream about,
Think about.
That boy with the baby face,
The poofy black hair,
The boy that is tall and has black eyes
That are so sweet,
    Who cares about you and you care about him.
That boy with the great personality,
    Who makes you laugh and giggle
        when you're feeling down and blue.
That boy that is fun to be around and with.
That boy that gives you his shoulder to cry on,
Maybe one day I'll find that boy,
And I'll know he was meant for me.

—Chari Heard

Wipe Out

You know that old saying "Step on the crack, break your momma's back!" I have a new one that would fit perfectly with me at the time: "Step on the crack, make yourself go SMACK!"

I was walking along the sidewalk one day, taking in all my surroundings and smelling spring scents and seeing new houses being built, trees being planted, and dust flying into my eye. All of a sudden I arrived at a street. I glimpsed a ways and saw or heard nothing coming. I decided to cross the street. I started to hear a car racing down the street so I took off running to get to the other side. I made it across, but when I got to the side walk, I noticed a crack that was never there before. I tried to stop running, but I couldn't. That's when it happened: I tripped. I started to see the sidewalk get closer and closer to my face. I ended up sliding on my face. I heard a large SMACK as I hit the ground.

I could hear kids running toward me. They took me to the nearest house. Come to find out it was my friend Jasmin's house. Jasmin took me in and called my mom to come and get me. About five minutes later my mom arrived. She raced me home. She tugged me inside, and got me a warm wash rag to wipe off my face. Then she comforted me. After that I went into the bathroom and looked into the mirror and cried, "I'M UGLY!" My face was all messed up. I had bruises, cuts, scrapes, a fat lip, and a black eye.

If you are walking on the sidewalk and you see a crack, step over it!

—Alexandra Tinsley

The Terrible Ship

Dear Journal,   February 10, 1789

I will never forget the one bright morning, when white men kidnapped my tribe. They enslaved us and forced us to walk many miles. They didn't give us very much food and never let us go to the bathroom without a white man there. I was extremely terrified!

We finally got to this large ship. We had to lie down on wooden shelves. I saw many grownups and children. I could feel the sadness of their families.

We started to move very slowly. I could smell and taste the salt of the ocean. I tried to move from the squishiness of everybody piled onto the ship. One of the white men unhooked me from my rope that tied my feet and hands. He took out this long, black, wiry whip. He told me that if I ever tried to get away he would whip me. Then he told me to stand still. He took the long whip and slashed it against my back. The white man took me back to where I had been and laid me down and put a ring on my neck. I was so angry I cursed many times.

We were half way to our destination when many people got seasick and vomited everywhere. My brother beside me had gotten sick from the ocean and accidentally vomited on me. I touched the vomit in disgust. It was across my stomach. I could taste it. It tasted like salt, when it gets out of the ground. I could also smell it. It smelled like salt, cheetah dumpings and skunk all mixed together. I looked around, checking if any white men were watching. I tugged at my neck brace. It wouldn't come off.

After awhile, I turned to my brother to see if he was okay. I called his name. He didn't answer. I screamed to one of the white men, asking if he would help him. He unhooked my brother and dragged him like he didn't care at all. The white man told his captain my brother was dead. They threw him off the deck roughly. I cried very loudly for a long time.

Later on that day I woke up to the smell of burning coal and dead bodies. On the other side of me was a friend of mine with blood everywhere. I could smell the blood from his neck. I could also taste it. I was horrified about what they might do to me. I thought that if I lived I would honor my family.

Suddenly, a white man kicked my chest to see if I was good enough to sell. My chest began to bleed. I touched it and thought I would die. I got mad and broke the ropes along my hands. Then I untied the rope on my feet. Many white men tackled me like they were going to murder me. They took a knife and stabbed me. They then forced me in a small, strange chamber. It took many weeks until this horrible journey was over.

This experience will have an effect on my life until I die. But as I have said, I will not give up. I will honor my family and their love for me.

Sincerely,
Kunta

—Alexis Bond

Winter
> The silence felt like death
> As I looked upon the view.
> Trees were bare
> With no color and hatred,
> And screaming with loneliness
> Within.
> No laughter, no music

Or colorful nature,
Only frozen ice and deathly cold
Closing in.
Will next season bring laughter again?
—Thao Van

The Forbidden Street

She looked right again
Before she crossed the forbidden street.
Her parents told her
Not to go across Amature Street,
But they didn't know the full
Content of how many liberties
She had discovered and taken before that.
She skipped school,
Phoning in sick using her mother's voice,
A new talent...
She hung out with new friends
Who got her to try her first cigarette.
Thirteen years old,
And she shoplifted for the first time.
Fourteen,
Her parents put her in rehab.
Now fifteen,
She tries to change her reputation
Back to innocent perfection,
But knows she can't as she
Tries in vain.
Time killed is time
Wasted,
And now she can't
Turn the clock back.

She can't get a real job,
Can't support herself
Because of everything
She did, starting from
The first rule
Broken,
Crossing the forbidden street.

—Rachel Staudte

Someone I'll Never Forget

My indelible moment was when my Uncle Mickey died. He was fifty-eight years old. I was really mad when he died, because he was my favorite uncle. I wish he were still here because I really miss him. I remember when I always went over to his house to help him clean it and feed his dogs. Plus, I would make him something to eat. Before he died, he bought me a watch for my birthday. I will never forget him asking what I wanted for my birthday. After my uncle passed away, I didn't eat for two days because I was so depressed.

My uncle was awesome. He always bought me what I wanted for Christmas. If he had a cat that had a litter of kittens, he would let me have one for free, or if he had a dog that he had to get rid of, he would let me have it. I will never forget the time he let me have a newborn kitten. The cat was reddish orange and named Fireball because he looked like a little red puffy ball.

I learned a lot from my Uncle Mickey. One thing he taught me was my A-B-C's. He said he had a picture of me writing them. I would like to see that picture. My uncle lived right next door to my grandma. Now, when I go to my grandma's house, I look over at my uncle's house, but he's never there. Even though he's gone, his absence does not mean he is not going to be in my heart. My life has changed because I'm used to going to his house and seeing him and helping with these things. I wish he would have lived longer to be there for more of my birthdays.

—Tara Wood

Adjustments

"MAKE HER STOP!" I yelled at my mom. My one year-old sister, Kiaira, or Kiki for short, wouldn't stop crying over a green bomb pop. Like most teens, I wanted all of the attention. Your first guess would be that having a new sibling would drag all of the attention from you to the newly born sibling. For example, you might want to do something, but you can't tell your mom because she is busy with the baby, work, or whatever, and she never has time for you. You're also afraid to ask her because she might get angry. She could turn into a mad dog with foam coming out her mouth! No matter what, she will just tune you out, right?

There are two solutions to this situation. One road, the good road, has nice results at the end. This road is taken by talking with your parents, and working out a family plan. The plan works only if you hold up your end of the agreement, like not fighting with siblings, or listening when talked to. Rules can also be set to the parents, like spending time with both you and your siblings separately. The other road, the bad road, is a road of selfishness. Once you're on that road, it is hard to change. You don't appreciate things you should appreciate, such as your own room, a place to escape, your own stereo, and friends that are your very own, not to mention parents that love you, and a very special sister.

This trip with the baby might be tremendously horrifying. You know things may not be the same. During the pregnancy, your mom will probably become tired, grouchy, and impatient. You begin to wonder if she will stay this way forever. So, finally your mother has the baby, and after a few months you realize that the baby is a thief. Before the baby was born, you were a wanted criminal for love. Now you are out on bond, and there is no point even trying to get noticed.

After a few months, you start to warm up to the baby. There are still things you didn't want to change, but they had to for the baby to adjust. You miss the peace and quiet at night, which is now replaced by earsplitting crying at 2:00. It might be a school night, so the next morning, you're grumpy. You miss the free time, too. Now all your free time that was yours before the baby is now taken up by helping your mom with the baby and doing your mom's house work. The list goes on and on.

Then suddenly, it's here! The baby's first birthday, and your mom has invited the whole universe, even the people from Mars.

WAIT! STOP! FREEZE! You're probably thinking I'm about to complain about how the baby's first birthday was treacherous, and how I wasn't noticed, etc., etc. Well, I actually liked it. Okay, I loved it! For the first time my baby sister said something, and it was to me! It was like she was reading my mind ever since she was born, and now she was sorry for all of the trouble she had caused me. Her smile and that two-syllable word made me regret every single bad word I had said about her. That day, I apologized for my mistakes, too.

Having a new brother or sister is not the only adjustment you'll have to deal with in your lifetime. Life is full of adjustments! Through all of this, even though it was a crazy, wild, brain blowing experience at times, I learned that you just go with the flow and plan ahead of time for those changes if possible. Trust me, it'll help you to not go crazy when the unexpected happens.

—Kaitlyn Seats

MOM

Although I had an ache
I was happy to be home.
As she stepped out of the car
My face turned bright.
I ignored my ache
And ran through the gate,
Threw my arms around her waist.
My journey ended
Finally
Because I had my mom.

—Adam Carr

Life Goes On...

It was 2:59, right when the bell rang. "Yes! School is out!" I said. I got my stuff, quickly ran outside, and started walking home just as Mom had told me to. Then I turned around and saw my mom sitting in the car. I ran to it and got in. All was silent. Nobody said a word. I remembered how my day had gone and how grandpa had been on my mind all day. I knew something was wrong. Mom started to turn around and I asked, "Why did you pick me up?"

She said, "Wait a minute, let me talk." She wanted to talk to me! The whole day had been bad, so I just knew what she had to tell me was going to be bad, too. My brother, Rick, continued driving toward Grandma and

Grandpa's house. Mom said, "Today, around five after twelve, your grandpa passed away."

I turned my head, looked out the window and cried and cried and cried. It just didn't seem real. Grandpa had always been there, always. He was our family's anchor that held us together and made sure everything went smoothly. But not anymore; he was gone, gone forever and no one could change that. I kept crying, crying, and crying.

We pulled up in grandma's driveway. My mom said, "Get out and go on in." She and my brother did, but I needed some time to myself, so I stayed in the car. My heart was torn as I sat there and cried. I held my coat close to me and buried my face in it. "Why did this happen to me?" I thought. The whole day made sense now. That's why I had been so depressed; that's why I wanted to be alone; that's why God placed those friends in my life, to help me get through it all.

I heard the car door open, so I raised my head up and saw that my mom's friend, whom I called Aunt Sue, was standing there. She got in the car and held me as I cried. She really missed Grandpa too because he had been like a dad to her. She began crying, too. Even though I wanted to be alone, I admit I was glad Aunt Sue was there.

My heart was pounding, and inside I felt like all of the joy, happiness, and love had been crushed and shattered into pieces of hate. I sat there crying, hating that he had died, hating he was gone, hating that he would never return. I stopped crying and lifted my head, and Aunt Sue said, "Let's go in." I knew I would have to do it sooner or later, so I went ahead and faced it.

I walked in, and Grandpa's chair wasn't there. Everything was moved around, and it was like reality had hit me all over again. I started crying and ran outside, got in the car, buried my face in my coat and cried like a baby until I fell asleep.

I woke up and my Aunt Margie from Tulsa was there. I must have slept for at least three hours. I looked at the clock, and I had been asleep for three hours and forty-five minutes. I ran inside and sat next to Aunt Margie and looked around and began accepting what had happened. I looked around and saw all the empty space and thought to my self, he's gone. Gone today, gone tomorrow, gone forever, but he's no longer suffering. I had to open up and cry and let my family hold me.

Through out all of this, I learned that it's okay to cry, but not to dwell on it forever. Grandpa wouldn't have wanted that at all. I still cry at the grave site sometimes, but I know he's no longer suffering, and so I've learned to move on with life.

Grandpa meant a lot to me. He was like the dad I never had. He taught me about the good things in life and good survival advice, like if Grandma isn't happy, just turn up the TV and ignore her. Same thing goes for Mom. He told me that just because I don't have something I want or I think I have to have, I shouldn't think life won't go on and be fun. He always said money isn't an issue in life that really matters. The only thing that matters is family and friends. He taught me that it's okay to be yourself, to be a little wild, to be crazy, and to have fun! Sometimes it's okay to spend more money than we should, and sometimes we should go out to eat even when it's cheaper to cook because life is short, so we should make the best of it! Spend it with friends and family, spend it cracking jokes, having burping contests, being yourself. Be the way God created you. Make the best of it!

—Racheal Hawthorne

Grandpa's Field
I was in my grandpa's field
One summer night,
Listening to the music
From the barn owls, crickets,
And frogs by the creek.
I looked at the moon
And saw the nighthawks
After moths.
That night so beautiful...
I never will forget.

—Randy Bradshaw

I Don't Know Why
You say you hate me,
I don't know why.
You say you never want to see me,
I don't know why.
You say you're going to kill me,
I don't know why.
I don't understand
Why you say these hurtful things.
Why say you hate me?
I do nothing to you.
Why say you don't love me?
I love you.
Why would you cut yourself?
Why? Why?
Would you cry yourself to sleep?
It's so sad to hear you cry.
Why would you sneak out and be gone for days?
Why? Why?

Did you kill yourself then?
I forgave you!
It's okay!
Why? Why?
I don't know why...

—Janessa McCafferty

Moonlit Pond

I wander by the moonlit pond,
Looking across the shadows,
Searching for myself, my soul.
I feel as if I'm lost
All of a sudden.
I run through the
Weeds of my childhood,
For I know I left it at
The moonlit pond.
When I come back it shall be there,
Waiting for my children.
I know it won't be the same,
But my happiness and carefree spirit
Will always be.
And whenever I go to my moonlit pond,
Looking across the shadowed field,
I will always know that twenty years ago, I was here,
Searching for my lost soul.

—Kristain Marsh

Deserted Highway

Following the endless, deserted highway,
Brightening stars above with a dying glow to the rest,
No taillights ahead of you to draw your mind away,

Or headlights to bring you back again.
    Down the open mirage of life,
You try to walk away from the past yet fail to gain the
future,
    Only seeing the here and now,
    With what you wish walking right beside you.
    One cannot listen, but only talk,
    When the other cannot talk, but only listen.
    The deepening darkness cloaks the cool waters of a
forgotten lake. As you walk your mind is fixed with the
past as it rambles on;
    You don't want to listen to what it says because you
wish things were different.
    But as they keep talking, you start to accept that it will
never change.
    The talking one sees you're thinking and knows.
    With a slight nod he turns around and disappears.
    You walk on with the silent one and start to talk, talk-
ing about anything that comes to mind, about your past
and about things you hope for and want to see.
    After a while of talking the silent one nods and walks
ahead of you, then disappears. The stars start to slowly go
out while the moving sun rises.
    Before the sun can hit the horizon, you turn around
and walk the way you came.

—Jessica DeMalia

Saturday
Saturday is a bright beautiful blue,
The color of a painted sky.
Saturday feels like flying on the wings of a giant bird;

It sounds like a radio playing Lynyrd Skynyrd and the
Allman Brothers.
It sounds like bonfires and motorcycles.
Saturday tastes like a half pound burger from Hardee's.
Saturday gives an awesome break from the long week
behind.

—Jessica DeMalia

Normandy

June in Normandy,
Peace, you would think.
But this journey is long,
The enemy is near.
The silence is broken
By the snap of a rifle.
Peace is gone;
The battle is now.

—Chris Haller

Deal With It

Do you ever wonder why people, especially parents, cry
and whine over things that make no sense? I don't know,
but I have a pretty good idea. People go around making
plans for the future, but when it comes, they are clueless.
The thing is, you can't plan for the future. Sure you can jot
some stuff down on paper, like go to the beauty school, get
a car and buy a house. Really, when it comes to it, your pri-
orities are at a hundred percent and your money is at thirty.

Whining is my definition of pouting, and that's just
what people do. They go around pouting all day until they
get it through their heads that no one is coming to rescue
them or give them a million dollars and say everything's
going to be okay. Why are you like that, you ask? I don't

know. That's just the way I am.

Crying comes from pain or emotions. The only time I think someone should cry over something is when it's serious, like getting your hand chopped off or a relative dying. I hate it when people cry over breaking a nail, getting a splinter in their foot, or just any little thing.

I think people should live their lives wisely instead of just crying or whining over things they cannot accomplish. I am sure everyone will say they can accomplish their dreams and wishes, but life does not work out the way you plan it. All I do is take what I get and live with it. I'm sure you have heard that before.

So instead of dreaming for things and not getting them, find something worthwhile that might make you happier in the future. You should get an education and a job before you start wanting things and not getting them in the future. Take what you get, and then you can start dreaming.

                                                        —Jenna Roan

My First Day of Sixth Grade

During the summer before sixth grade, I was so excited because I was going to middle school. I was telling everyone about my excitement. I was so excited that I felt like getting up and dancing.

Then it came, the night before school. I could not get to sleep. I was too excited! I had to take a Benadryl because I couldn't get to sleep, but I was still up and down all night. Before I knew it, it was morning. I was rushing my mom to go. When I got to school, I was shivering because I was so nervous. But the weird thing was that I wasn't even tired from not getting any sleep. I guess I was just so excited that I couldn't even be sleepy, and besides, the day had only begun.

When I got inside, I headed for the gym. You could only go to the cafeteria or the gym. When I was walking down the hallway, you could hear the basketballs bouncing. When you walked in, you could smell the cologne and the perfume that all the boys and girls were wearing. You could even smell the shampoo and the conditioner. The scent smelled so good. It was like a whole bunch of fruit filled the room.

I was looking for my friend, and all of a sudden I spotted her. As I walked across the basketball court it felt like all the people were watching me. I felt kind of scared because I don't like it when people are just staring at me. When I got to Nicole, I felt so much better. Nicole and I started talking. She was really excited about middle school, too. Then just as our other friends walked in, the bell rang.

My first class of the day was English and reading. When I walked in the room, I could hear pencils writing and the air conditioner running. I could see the blinding sun coming through the window. For some reason, the room smelled like peaches. The teacher's name was Mrs. Gagnon. She had long, blond, brown hair.

Next was science. When I walked into Mrs. James's room you could smell the heavy perfume she was wearing. You could see the posters that she had hung up over the summer, and of course, the assignment on the board. It was the "Do Now." She read some important stuff out of our student handbook. Mrs. James was really funny, but you could get on her bad side!

My last class of the day was math. When I walked in I could see the math posters with factors and stuff like that on them. I could see the math binders and also see the math books that we would be using that year. Right when I walked in, I could feel the sweat dripping down my face because of the blazing hot sun at 1:15 in the afternoon. The teacher, Mrs. Lane, luckily had a good sense of humor!

The rest of the day I didn't get lost, and I didn't even have any homework. I was glad I had made it to all my classes on time. I liked all my teachers right away. I knew it would be a good year; it had been so far. My dad picked me up after school, and I told him that I had a great first day of school. I will always remember my first day of middle school.

—Savannah King

At My Grandma's House

I was just getting out of my car, and I could already smell the rich smell of brownies in the oven coming from Grandma's house. I could see my uncle next door walking toward us to greet us. As I was coming in, I could feel the cold doorknob. Inside, the sofa felt so soft and the vases with flowers were beautiful.

I could see all the pretty colors on Grandma's dress. The smell of the popcorn my brothers were eating mixed with the smell of the fresh air from outside and all the dust from the cars driving by. I could hear my cousins playing in the back yard and I could already taste the brownies in my mouth. When Grandma offered me some, they were delicious! I could barely think of anything else but how delicious they were, as brown as mud and really warm, just out of the oven. They were delectable.

I hope that when I grow up my grandma will still be alive so I can visit her every Christmas and every summer of my life. I love going over to my grandma's house—home of the best brownies ever!

—Abby Fernandez

JARRETT MIDDLE SCHOOL

The Tears Poured Out

My cousin Andelin was so awesome. She was my favorite cousin and the greatest person I have ever met. She had so many wonderful talents. She went to a culinary arts school, she was an awesome artist, and she was a very strong Christian. She was the kind of person you would meet and talk to once, and you would love her.

About ten years ago, when I was three, Andelin was diagnosed with Lupus. Lupus is an autoimmune disease in which your body attacks itself. Andelin suffered a long battle, but somehow she still remained positive. She never had any negative thoughts. Even though Andelin was sick, she always volunteered to help at her church. She put on an amazing circus for the children; she was the ringmaster, and all the children thought she was real.

On the morning of January 21, 2005, the phone rang just after my alarm clock went off. I sat up in my bed and my mom answered the phone. I just had a gut feeling that it was about Andelin. I jumped out of my bed, ran into my parents' room, and asked what was wrong. My mom said that Andelin had passed away early that morning. My heart stopped. The tears just poured out of my eyes. I've never seen my dad that upset. Then my dad went and told my sister. The four of us just sat on my parents' bed and cried for a long time.

In the past five years I have lost five close relatives. Yes, it was hard and sad, but they had had a long life and were older. Andelin was only thirty-three. Toward the end of Andelin's life, her body and spirit no longer matched. She was so weak that she couldn't fight any more.

I believe God used her to touch many people's lives. What I don't understand is why He couldn't have made her better and let her continue to touch lives. Andelin was so faithful, she has inspired me to be a better person.

—Kayla Grouch

Life

All my life, I've always wondered what it would be like to have a normal life. My mother just recently passed; she committed suicide. She left a note saying that life was just too hard to bear. I will always love her, but I will never forgive her for the pain she has put my brother and me through.

I feel like there is no one who knows how I feel and what I have been through. I feel like I am an adult, and yet I'm only thirteen years old. No one ever talks to me about her death, especially people in my family. That's why I feel so alone.

I just thought I might let all of you readers out there

know that life might get hard, but never give up! I used to dream at night hoping that life would turn out better, but my dreams never came true. Sometimes I'm amazed that I have made it this far; but I still have so much life ahead of me.

I have made it my goal in life not to end up like my mother. I plan to make a life for myself. I plan to finish high school; my mother only made it to tenth grade. After high school I plan to go to college and start a career. Those are my goals.

Let me give you some advice. Life is going to get hard, but you can always work through it.

—Linsie Long

Backstabbing Buds

Do you have a friend who talks bad about you and just tries to start fights? I do, and yet I still call her a friend. I don't understand why.

She knows everything about everyone, and if she doesn't have dirt on someone, she will make it up. Everyone is scared of her; they don't say it, but they are. She has this power over all of my friends; and she talks about them. Worst of all, I hate to admit it, but she talks about me, too. She probably even talks about you!

The problem with her is there are so many people just like her. Slowly but surely I'm turning into her and so are my friends; however, we just refuse to see it. She is so good at what she does, she even gets out of detentions and I.S.S. If adults don't see it, how are we supposed to? It's just a teenage problem with backstabbing buds.

—Janelle Grimm

Blind To My Cry
> I show all the signs, but everyone's blind.
> I scream all the time, but no one can hear.
> I'm trapped up inside, but no exit is near.
> I try to tell you, but you're never here.
> I scream at myself just to hide from the fear.
> I show all the signs, but everyone's blind.
>
> —Alex Love

School
> *School, everyone thinks it's such a bore,*
> Telling us stories that make us snore.
> The social cliques of preps and jocks,
> Also the teachers that really rock.
> We never have a pencil or a pen,
> But we all know how to count to ten.
> We all have some kind of nickname,
> The soccer team puts the football team to shame.
>
> School, everyone thinks it's such a bore,
> But I know ours is solid to the core.
>
> —Rudy Fotsch

The Pimple
There once was a girl with a really big zit,
> When people saw her they cringed a little bit.

> A mean boy told her, "You've got a zit up there!
> It's so red it almost matches your hair!"

When she got home she ran to the mirror.
"If only my face were a little bit clearer!"

On her nose was a zit, at the very tip top.
She got up all her courage, squeezed it, then . . .
POP!

—Anna Withers

My Feelings
When I'm around my best friend,
I am a kid in a candy store,
Thrilled and hyper.
When I'm around my parents,
     I am a sloth,
     Pitiful and slow.

When I'm around my boyfriend,
I'm a dog about to be taken on a walk,
     Happy and overjoyed

When I'm by myself,
I'm a little lost puppy,
Lonely and bored.

When I'm at school,
I'm a car without gas,
Unable to work.

When I'm at the mall,
I'm a tiger finding its dinner,
Ready and going.

When I'm tired,
I'm a sponge without water,
Stiff and unmoving.

When I'm playing volleyball,
I'm a shark chasing a fish,
Fast and committed.

—Katie Batterson

PIPKIN MIDDLE SCHOOL

Stars

We stare at the stars at night,
Sometimes on a romantic date,
Sometimes to contemplate our fate;
But as I gaze at the stars,
I wonder if they're looking back.

I wonder if the stars can see
The children abandoned on the street,
The mothers working two jobs,
The men fighting for our country.

I wonder if the stars can see me,
The lonely boy walking down the street,
If they can see me
Trying to find my way through,
If they can help me just once.

If the stars see us,
 I wonder if they can see a glow,
As we see in them.
If only the stars can see us.

—Shawn Tetlow

Divorce

My heart is torn to pieces...
How many pieces do I have left?
Not many.
I know 'cause it took
A big chunk away.
My eyes well with tears as I
Mourn over the thought
That the moment my parents
Split I knew the loneliness was coming.
How long does it have to go on,
My loneliness and despair?
I don't know how many tears I have left to shed
But...
The question is, why?

—Brittany Chilson

Happy Times

Happy days,
Happy times,
Life isn't what you want it to be.
Love, life, laughter,
Now all we need is peace!

—Eleni Elliott

The Long Walk of Life
Where the wind whistles through the weeping willows,
That's where peace is.
Where the woeful wanderer finally finds his home,
That's where his heart is.
When all mankind is finally unified,
You will find what you seek.
When you find peace, your home, your heart,
Your journey will have met its end.
                                        —Ashley Mitchell

My Bad Luck Show and Tell
My show and tell in the third grade brought bad luck to only two people—Gary Gibbles and me!

For my show and tell, we had to go outside. I showed my porcelain doll, an Indian purse my dad made, and my tennis racket given to me when I made Regionals. I was about to hit the tennis ball when I heard someone scream in agony and pain, but I kept going like nothing had happened.

When we arrived inside, all I heard was commotion. I saw a blue/purple welt on Gary's neck, and I asked what had happened. That's when I was told his story and then understood why there was such a commotion.

As I was giving my show and tell, there was a drive-by paint ball shooting, and Gary got shot in the neck with a paint ball. That's why I've never given another show and tell outside since. I'm afraid it will bring nothing but bad luck!
                                        —Meagan Tosh

The Thing—A Daydream

On a hot scorching summer day in July, I saw a picture, a marvelous picture, a golden picture of a dragon. A dragon with sharp claws, teeth like daggers, long wings, and a large body with things unimaginable. There were also volcanoes in the picture, erupting and disintegrating things like a tornado in a tube. The people in the picture were panicking because of the dragon and the lava from the volcanoes. There I was in the picture looking like a dummy and looking like my soul was taken away. Suddenly, I came back to reality and moved out of the way just in the nick of time. I almost died right there.

When I moved, I was awakened, but found my imagination was turned on. The picture had been so real when things started happening, but now people started looking at me. I told them it was just my imagination. The daydream was fun and adventurous, but I don't want it to happen again, not even in my night dreams! It happened all too quickly, and it almost seemed like a nightmare. I don't like nightmares!

—Nate Cawlfield

To Whom It Concerns

To whom it concerns:
I hate my life;
I feel like I have too much.
To whom it concerns:
I don't get any boys' looks
(They never look at the tomboys.)
To whom it concerns:

I'm doing this for attention.
To whom it concerns:
I feel like I'm a bug nobody likes.
To whom it concerns:
My life is a lie.
To whom it concerns:
Goodbye

—Jennifer Napieralski

REED
MIDDLE
SCHOOL

Football: A True Passion

As I sit all alone in my blue and gold rocking chair, in front of my trophy wall, I think about my past experiences with football, and all the great things it has brought to me. I remember sitting on my couch with my father, screaming, hollering, cheering, and rooting for our team. My favorite football team when I was a young child was the St. Louis Rams. They were, and are, my idols.

I remember not understanding the wonderful sport of football, but still liking to watch it with my father. I didn't understand football until I got into the second grade, when I moved into John B. Hughes, an apartment complex on Clifton Avenue. I played with kids two and three years older than me; therefore, I got hurt a lot. One time I even got into a fight for tackling a kid so hard that his head bounced off the ground! He didn't like that very well!

When I started understanding football better, I played even more. I was hungry for the sport. The physicality of it was my favorite reason to play. I liked tackling people as hard as I possibly could, making them hurt, as well as myself!

My father, being disabled, couldn't afford for me to play Mighty Mites, but when I got to seventh grade, I played for my school, Reed Middle School. I was a first string player, and I started every game at right guard or right tackle. For my defensive positions, I started at right defensive tackle.

During the fifth game of the year, as I stood in my fire out position on the football field, all I could hear was the crowd going wild, and voices in my head telling me not to let the team down, to hit the other guy hard. But far off in the background, I could hear my father saying, "Just do your best. That is all you can do." Those were the words that motivated me. Those words led me to the place I am now. That night, with an excellent quarterback, Sam Smith, and a quick center, Aaron Abercrombie, we won Reed's second ever Seventh Grade Division Championship.

Football is my greatest passion.

—Houston Gould

Babysittin' Blues

Have you ever baby sat before? If you have, I so totally respect you! Babysitting is hard work with very little play. I would like to tell all you babysitting gals out there a little story about the first time I ever babysat. I was to babysit a little boy named Cain, with my older sister.

When we got to Cain's house, my sister started to

watch a movie, *A League of Their Own*. Cain wanted to go outside, so guess who had to take him? That's right, me. Then Cain wanted to watch a movie. Guess who had to start it for him? That's right, me. When Cain got hungry, guess who had to feed him? Me. After all this, when Cain went to bed, guess who had to put him in bed? Me. I did all this while Sarah just sat there, watching me.

After Cain's parents got home, it was time for the best part: getting paid! It turns out Sarah was paid $10, and all I got was $5. Of course I got mad, but Sara said she did everything. Think about it—who's a mom going to believe, a little 10-year-old or the "more responsible" 12-year-old? Even though all that happened, it still ended well. I now baby-sit all the kids alone, and I get all of the cash. Sarah doesn't babysit at all. Go figure.

Now if you have just started babysitting, I have a few tips for you.

#1: If the kids start acting up, don't be afraid to put them in time-out for a while.

#2: Always keep an eye on the little ones. You never know what they could do or where they could go!

#3: If they want you to do something with them, just do it! If you don't, they tend to get a little upset!

#4: Just have fun. Learn from this story, and you just might become the best babysitter ever.

—Stephanie Urrutia

Alone

> Cold, sitting here all alone, no one around, no sound.
> No love, no hate, just the wind on my back.
> I cry as the loneliness attacks.
> I ran away, hoping for you to come.
> I hope some one can save me.
> The darkness overcomes.
> I realize I can't go back home.
> Help me please; I'm cold, lost, and all alone.
>
> —Heather Roach

True Friends

A true friend is a person you can call at four in the morning, to whom you can spill out your heart. A true friend is someone you can tell all your secrets and know, without a shadow of a doubt, that your secrets are safe. I think everybody comes across his or her true friends eventually, but maybe lets them go without knowing. I have had my true friend forever. She has always been there for me. She is not your typical childhood best friend, however. She is 73 years old, plump, and gray haired. She is my grandmother.

I can talk to her about anything, and I do. She will always do her best to help me when I need her, or cheer me up when I am down. She may not always have the answers, but she always knows what to say to make her granddaughter feel better.

I remember one time when I was staying the weekend with her, when my mom called to tell us some bad news. I answered the phone, only to hear my mom sobbing on the other line. She wanted to talk to Grandma. I listened to my grandmother's end of the conversation, trying to find out what was going on, but I had no clues. After hanging up, my grandmother, fighting back tears, told me what happened: my brother had run away. Immediately, I started crying. My grandma comforted me, telling me that it would all be okay. After about three hours of waiting nervously, my mom called back, and once again Granny was right. The police had found my brother, and he was okay.

Another time was when my granddad was in the hospital with only a week or two to live. He had been having heart surgery when he had a stroke, causing him to be in a coma until the day he died. We all went to the hospital and took turns staying with Grandma to comfort her. After seeing Granddad's lifeless-looking body hooked up to thousands of tubes, we were all devastated, including Granny, but she stayed strong. She is the strongest person I know. Eventually Granddad died. He was a very loved person, so we were once again all very sad, but Granny still stayed strong and helped us through it all. We were all with her to comfort her, but really she ended up comforting us.

Grandma has always been there for me, and she always will be until the day she dies. I have learned from her to be a better person. I hope I can be as good a grandma to my grandkids someday as she has been to me.

—Samantha Phillips

The Early Bird Gets the Worm

Have you ever heard the expression *the early bird gets the worm*? Well, do I have a funny story to tell you...

One early morning, I woke up before the rest of my

family. I got into the steaming hot shower for an hour. Then I got out of the shower, feeling fantastic. Later that morning, my sister Amanda woke up and got in the shower. I thought to myself, "Oops! I took all of the hot water!"

A couple of seconds later, I heard a thump. It was my sister. She had fallen, and yelled, "Dustin, I'm going to get you back!" When my sister came out of the bathroom, she was furious. She went and woke Mom up, and Mom proceeded to stomp across the house into my room. I tried to hide myself under the blanket while Mom shouted, "Don't torment your sister like that!" Amanda was hiding behind my mom, smirking. I wanted to yell at her!

The next morning, I woke up fairly early and noticed my sister playing videogames in the front room. I thought something was fishy because she never wakes up earlier than me. I went to my bedroom, got my clothes, and stepped in the shower.

I turned the knob suspiciously. I hesitated a moment, then turned on the shower. Suddenly, ice-cold water came gushing out! "Mandy!" I yelled, "That's not funny!" In the background, I heard my sister laughing with my mom. I learned a very important lesson that day: The early bird should share half the worm!

—Dustin Shanahan

The Day My Mom Saved My life

Around Easter a few years ago, the day was warm, and I was playing tag with one of my friends, Sarah, when we decided to run through the side yard. I was chasing her, when I guess I did not notice the glass on the ground, and I just kept running.

I was running at full speed, when suddenly I felt a

sharp pain in my right ankle. When I looked down, I saw all the blood. I dropped down, curled up holding my ankle, and started bawling my eyes out. My mom heard me and came out of nowhere. In her head she put it all together: the glass, the blood, and me. She rushed inside to get a damp towel and then wrapped it around my ankle to try and stop all of the bleeding.

The rest of my family came running to see what was going on. All I could hear was my mom flipping out, yelling, "Oh my god! You can see her bone! We've got to get her to the hospital, now!" At this point I was freaked out, but I also thought it was kind of cool that you could see my bone without any skin over it!

Later that day, at the hospital, I got 42 stitches and a whole bunch of candy. The doctor said I could've bled to death if we had waited any longer to go to the hospital. My mom was the hero of the day! I finally got to leave the hospital. After that, I'm not sure if my friend Sarah ever wanted to come back over to my house!

—Stephanie Hinkle

San Francisco

The best place I have ever lived is San Francisco. Every day I would wake up and go outside to find a warm, not hot, air, and people in bathing suits the colors of the rainbow. But the one thing that caught my eye was the ocean.

The ocean never changes in your heart. You can't see the bad, only the good. You can only see the sparkling blue water washing away the hot sand. You can just sit and think of all the living creatures in the ocean: fish, sharks, dolphins, sea snails, and more. It is a never-ending list of amazing animals and plants in the ocean. All you can see above is a mixture of white and blue water, unaware of what is really under there.

The ocean outside San Francisco is like a big world all its own, separate from the world on land. It is like a new planet being explored, and there is so much more to dream of.

Another thing that makes San Francisco the best place is the weather...how the weather stays warm enough so you never have to go inside. The sky is bright with sun rays of yellow and orange, always shining, keeping everything cozy. I could go outside and run for miles on the hot brown sand while the sun's rays would shine over me like a big orange and yellow blanket.

San Francisco is like Heaven to me—a place of warmth and new discoveries. That is why it is the best place I have ever lived.

—Jessica Jackson

Pretend

We were just a game
It wasn't real
We could never be together
We were like a one-month trend
Just pretend.

Everything, fake
Everything, just a lie
There was no love
Only two different people
Who weren't supposed to be:

You and me.

—Leah Bailey

Predator vs. Alien

As I walked down the dark corridor, I looked for my enemy. I was hunting the last alien inside the pyramid. My cloaking device was working as the elders had said it would. Spear in hand, I walked a little faster.

I saw the hunter's cloak refracting the light. My wounded arm dripped acidic blood. It sizzled as it hit the floor. My lips curled up. My goal was so close, and yet so far away.

A sizzling attracted my attention. The stone floor behind me was starting to melt. My gaze traveled up. On the ceiling was my foe, snarling at me.

My cloak had short-circuited when the alien jumped at me. Its tail came sweeping around and stabbed my shoulder. I howled in pain as my green blood oozed out of my wound. The creature went limp on my spear. I ripped its tail out of my arm.

I had left my mark. My life was almost depleted. My vision was growing dark. I knew I was already dead. My mind just refused it. My life was short, but...but...

—Jenna Briggs

My First Grade Year

Coming from lowly kindergarten, you take a big step— a step into first grade. It may be very different for other people, but for me, it was the best grade in elementary school, all because of a great teacher.

Ms. Hodgeson was her name. She looked to be in her mid-sixties. She was tall and carried a certain aura with her, indicating that she was very friendly.

Every day we were given lessons on spelling and grammar. The way Ms. Hodgeson taught made an impact on our lives. You see, she was different from any of my other teachers for this reason. She taught, but let us do the work in our own way.

Ms. Hodgeson had a rabbit named Sport, and we were allowed to play with him, as long as we put on Germ-X first. We also watched TV shows every day. One was about a boy named Arthur, and the other was about a little lemur. Next on our agenda, we would play a computer game that let us paint pictures and ultimately showed our creativity.

In general, first grade was a great year. Back in those old days, we all kicked it and had fun doing so. Every day was different, and I made a lot of friends, most of whom are with me today in middle school.

Ms. Hodgeson taught us lessons to live by. She taught all of her students things like good posture, which we can all use! She also taught us how to be polite, how to ask questions politely, which has helped stupendously. She described money and how to spend it wisely. She made each and every person feel that we had a purpose, and told us to be nice and courteous. Everything that she said has made a difference in our lives.

First grade year passed slowly, and then came the day when we had to move up to the second grade. The worst part about it was that Ms. Hodgeson was retiring! I found out from one of my mom's friends that she moved to Brooklyn, New York. I hope she and Sport are enjoying life in the big city. To this day, everything Ms. Hodgeson taught me greatly affects how I live my life.

—Matthew Stidham

My Dad (My Old Dad)

Where are you? Where have you been? Those are the questions that used to run through my head. That was when I was weak, but I'm stronger now. I don't need you.

Sometimes, when I was younger, I would cry myself to sleep, waiting, wondering when you would come back. You didn't come back, and for that I thank you. I thank you because we—my mom, your other son, and I—we have all moved on. We were strong, and now we don't need you.

Hate. Hate is a powerful word. It's a word I try not to use, but, in this case, it seems highly appropriate. I hate you! How could you leave us? I don't love you. That's something we must have in common. You probably don't even remember my birthday.

You know, I'm glad you're not in my life. You probably wouldn't be man enough to take care of me, or the rest of my family. There's another person in our lives now, my true dad. You're not my dad; you're my enemy. My dad loves me. You don't, but he does. Just remember, I'll continue to grow stronger. I don't need you. I never will.

You're probably in jail now. You're never there for me; you never were. I remember when I saw you for the first time. You stood 6'7", 280 pounds. I was speechless when we met. How could I say something to someone I hated so much? It's a good thing I don't have to go through that again. I never, and I do mean never, want to see you again.

I used to wish you would come back home some day. Don't ever, ever come back. Wishes, hopes, and dreams— that's all you ever were to me. No more, no less.

I'm better off without you. You've missed so much in my life...all of my birthdays, my grades, my girlfriends, everything. I'm strong, and I grow stronger every day. Just leave my family and me alone. Forever.

—Jacob Bittle

Mosquitoes

    These nasty insects, worse than flies,
    Will stare at you through big, round eyes!
    Their long thin bodies and narrow wings
    Contain a substance that makes their biting sting!

    They'll suck your blood through a needle-like nose,
    Sharply pointed like a poison dart that makes you doze!
    With spiny little legs they crawl on your skin,
    They truly are a "bug of sin!"

    Flying around and spreading disease,
    These putrid bugs make you feel unease!
    With their constant biting and annoying pain,
    Mosquitoes could drive someone sane insane!

—Karesse Wilkey

It's Just a CRAZY Day

          Cars on Mars
        Eating candy bars,
      It's just a CRAZY day.

        Dolls making calls
      While climbing up walls,
      It's just a CRAZY day.

Pigs wearing wigs
While playing with twigs,
It's just a CRAZY day.
—Ashley Lodwick

It Could Never Be
It could never be
Between you and me.
I tried to see
But could not breathe.

I hate our past,
The way it could not last.
I hate the way we fought before,
But it's my fault in the end.
Now you've come back again.
After all the pain
You've left a stain.

I hate the way the sky is blue,
The way it reminds me of you.
We're not one, but two;
I guess now you lose.

You and I could never be.
Why don't you see?
I hate the way you've left before,
Left me lying on the floor.
And when you said, "I love you,"
I hate thinking all was not true.

Now all is lost—
Now you know what love costs.

It can never be
Between you and me.

—Samantha Wiseman

CHEROKEE MIDDLE SCHOOL

The Importance of Family

Family is the most important thing in my life. Sure, I have friends. They're important to me too. But, throughout life they will come and go, depending on how significant the relationship is to me. They sometimes pass me by, but I will always have family.

When I need someone to express my feelings to by talking or if I need someone to confide in, my family is always there. When I'm feeling lonely and need someone to keep me company, guess who spends the day with me doing the fun things I want to do? My family does. Occasionally, I may find myself sick or feeling down, and they are still persistent in being there to comfort me and nurse me back to good health no matter how long it takes.

Providing food for me to eat, clothes to cover my back, and a shelter from the dangers of the world, is what they have graciously done all these years. Most of all, they ask me questions that are essential for every soul to hear, to ensure that they are important and their opinion actually means something. What do you want, what do you need, and what can we do to make your life better? They didn't just come right out and ask me these questions, but I could hear them through the way my parents raised me. A college fund and starter money are being saved up right now.

As these things were being done, where was I, when it was my turn to thank them or show them I loved them? I was out with my friends having fun, or locked in my room, never bothering to consider their feelings.

Now that I look back on how good my life was, I regret the way I was, ungrateful and selfish. I regret not saying a single thank-you or giving a hug or a kiss. Why do I have such a different perspective on life now? Well, it's because everything that I had is no more, including my family. Everything happened so fast, like a shooting star soaring beyond the heavens into nothingness. I never knew what I had and how valuable it was until I didn't have it anymore. The most important lesson that I learned from this was to love your family, and never be ashamed of who they are, who you are, or where you come from.

—Victoria Mitchell

Green Cities
 I sit at my window
 Watching the birds singing
 And the squirrels running
 Up the trees.
 Seasons pass, leaves change colors

And fall to the ground.
I feel imprisoned,
Trapped, with no way out.
My only hope is to reach
And escape to the outside,
Beyond my backyard....
To climb those trees, to smell
Those flowers, to jump in the
Piles of leaves.

I would sit in the grass
With the wind blowing my long hair.
The grass would tickle my feet
As I ran through it.
But all I ever see is the
Winding roads and tall buildings
Of the city with the gas choking
Me with every breath.
For now, the trees and the grasses
Are only my dream
Until I make it become reality.

—Amanda Lacey

Mirror Image
I look in the mirror
But do not recognize the
Person looking back at me.
I do not see the
Girl who once was on the
Soccer and baseball team.
I do not see the girl who

Did not care if her nail broke
Or if she got dirty.
I see a preppie cheerleader
In the "popular" crowd.
Is this me?
Is this who I want to be?
Will my other friends
Even accept me back again?
I know one thing.
I do not like my lifestyle right now.
I would rather be on the team
Than to be the one to watch them.
I want my life to change
Back to what it was before.
So in the hall,
I smile at my old friends
And they smile back.
Maybe there is a chance.
There is hope for me!
A spark has started.
I have a choice to make.
Maybe I can combine
Both lifestyles into a new one.
There is hope.
There is a goal.
There is a chance
That I must take.
Again I look in the mirror
And I smile back
At my reflection.

—Amanda Lacey

Far Away

    I used to think I was somebody,
    I used to be happy.
    Until the one fateful night,
    I found out I would never be the same.
    Sucked down into a black hole
    Of confusion and fright,
    Wondering what happened
    To my mother that night.
    Off in the distance I heard a faint noise,
    It made me wonder,
    Where was I?
    Everything looked white.
    I asked a man where my mother was;
    He said she went to the light.
    I knew from then on
    It would never be the same;
    I knew from then on,
    I would never see my mother again.
                        —Kathryn Ferdon

Friends Forever

"Jo, look out!" cried Lacey.

Bang! Crunch! Slip! Swoosh! Everything went black. I could only feel my body being lifted and my head throbbing. Finally, I opened my eyes; I wasn't outside, but in my family's living room.

I lifted my head off the floor, only to be forced back down by a sudden shot of pain that raced through my body. I laid my torn hand on my head and then pulled it away, only to reveal blood. My head was still throbbing, my legs felt like boards, my hands were sore, and my face felt as if it was on fire.

"You must have had a rough fall, Jo," said Dad, as he entered the room. He sat down beside me and changed the ice packs on my legs.

"Where's Lacey?" I croaked. Then I felt the clean chip across my front teeth, and another shot of pain ran through my body. I winced at the sudden pain.

"She is outside with her mother and Mom. We will be getting you in to the dentist first thing tomorrow. Also, Mom and I decided that you should take a break for tomorrow and stay home."

"But..." another shot of pain ran through my body. "Okay, you win," I replied weakly.

After a while, Lacey came in and told me what had happened after I blanked out. While she talked, I sat there quietly, munching on ice-chips.

"You must have lost control of your bike when you hit the gravel. Then, when you were on the ground, Mr. and Mrs. Hillman were walking and saw you crash, so they helped me take you home."

Crunch! Crunch! I nodded in agreement. Every time I touched my chipped teeth, they would send a shock of pain through my mouth. Chewing very carefully, I thought about the next couple of days that would await me.

The next day, I sat around the dentist's office, got my teeth fixed, and slept the rest of the day away. My caps felt funny at first and then I got used to them. I could only eat soft foods and I could not chew gum. My face was very tender, and everyone could tell where the new scabs were trying to grow in. My Mom and Dad were extra nice. They did their best to get me to take a nap, and nap I did!

That night I lay awake, knowing what the next day would bring. I wondered if I would be teased or shunned. The more I thought, the more unsure I became about going to school. The next thing I knew...Beep! Beep! Beep! My alarm went off; time to get ready to take on the day.

A half an hour later, I stood at the bus stop waiting for the bus to come roaring down the big hill. The November wind nipped at my face; I tugged at my sleeves, trying to keep my body heat inside. Then the bus showed up and screeched to a halt. I slowly boarded. All eyes and sounds of shock came when I revealed my beaten up face. It was the beginning of a long day.

The day was a cold and dreary one. In the halls, I was shot "unsure" and "you look awful" looks. Also, behind by back, I could hear "scab face" "ugly" and "beaten up piece of scum." I dragged myself to all my classes, one after another. My friends held up my head that morning and each teacher gave me a bright smile, as if to say that it was going to be okay.

Then the next thing I knew, I was on my way home. I laid my head back and the thoughts of home filled my mind. Then, a snotty voice called me back to reality. "Hey scab face!" my evil enemy since the fourth grade shouted. What she had against me, I had no clue. I opened my mouth to respond, but someone cut me off.

"Hey! Leave Jo alone; she has done nothing to you! I think she might just look better than you do, even when she looks beaten up!"

One of my best friends, Rande, was staring right into the girl's eyes. With one big huff, "the enemy" turned around to her so-called "group." Rande could only smile at her victory.

"Thanks."

"No problem. Someone has to give her a taste of her own medicine sometime or later." We both laughed. "If you need someone to lean on, or someone to brush you off, I will always be there." Somehow, from that point on, I knew I would be okay.

—Casandra Renschler

To Begin Again

A startling part of life learning is that it takes so long to realize some of the simplest concepts life teaches. Indeed, life throws so very many obstacles into my path that at times I completely forget what I once knew so well. It does not matter...I will always relearn the most important lesson of all: Once you have fallen, you must always rise up, ready to begin again. I understand completely the meaning of this timeless sentiment.

Grief comes in all sorts of forms. But it is of no consequence which way it hurts us, whether it is mild, or a wrenching blow, grief will always cause an ache within the heart. For me, grief came when I made the transition to Cherokee Middle School. I truly felt as if I had fallen. However, with time, life taught me that I could not stay down forever. I stood once more, and began again. That was one of the most important lessons I have ever been taught.

Struggles come and go for everyone. There is no person in the world who will not find herself isolated in grief at some point in her life. The lesson is learned again and again for everyone. No matter how hard or often people fall, they must always rise once more, ready to begin again. There are many lessons that I as a young individual am learning...but I know this completely about life: I must always rise again.

—Anisha Rimal

(This is dedicated to all those trying to overcome the fire of addiction.)

The Monster

I step out of my corner,
Out of the shadows,
Past the border
Of a line I dared not cross
For the longest TIME.

What lies past the border
Is the longest road I've ever traveled,
Yet it seems it made my life shorter.
I watched myself unravel,
And I could do NOTHING.

I stand at one end of the room
And stare into the other;
As everything flashes back,
I feel the urge
And I start to CRACK.

I reach for the monster
Which was once my friend,
But now I know;

Never again will it be my friend...
Not ever, not even in the END.

My hand feels frozen in time.
I think back to what it's cost me,
But still, it hurts me to say
That when I start to climb,
I begin to SLIP.

I can already feel
The overcrowding thoughts,
Starting to make my head reel...
And don't believe what I have started,
But I begin to peel AWAY.

I feel so far away,
So high and away from the pain.
I feel everyday I wake,
Away from all of my problems...
I just wish I could've solved THEM.

Before it came to this,
I don't even know who I am anymore,
(Not like I knew me before)
But I feel the worst part coming...
I can't even start RUNNING!

Where do you go
To run away from yourself?
I can't even escape from my mind;
And I realize,
I'm trapped in this living HELL.

The monster starts in my mouth,
Then it burns,
Coursing through every one of my veins.
I won't ever learn
How it causes so much PAIN.

Mixed emotions all in motion,
Blurred in an endless ocean
Of my darkest fears...
I try to blur through the fog,
But still nothing seems to CLEAR.

I begin to break down,
And I begin to drown
In the demon that is me;
Then there is a pause,
As I try to break FREE.

The monster fights back,
But I fight too;
It comes back for more,
But I say "no,"
And I have broken THROUGH.

I draw back my hand
From where it stood,
And look at the monster;
All of the demon in me
DISSOLVES.

The monster still fights,
It cries and cries,

"One more can't hurt,
Come on and give it
A TRY."

I look at the demon,
I look at the monster
And reach for it and throw it in the fire,
And I say to myself,
Once more, "You can"—and it's my voice...
It's my CHOICE.

—Cayleigh Medina Arens

Experiences

As years progress and hair turns gray, life's little lessons remain in one's mind forever. I have made many mistakes throughout the years, errors I have learned from. These lessons have helped me progress and grow in life. Most of these lessons, although simple and slightly ridiculous, have helped me become a better person.

At a young age, I made many mistakes that led to valuable lessons. Although these lessons were somewhat silly and juvenile, they helped me learn the consequences of my actions. Among the most memorable of these childhood mistakes were the following: cat food, as yummy as it looks on television, does NOT taste as good as people food; pinch someone in the arm and he will probably pinch you back; and never tell your mom her new diet is not working out!

However, the older I got, the more valuable the lessons became. Through many difficult and heartbreaking experiences, I learned that friendship is truly the most important possession I can own. I have also learned always to listen to what my mom is trying to tell me. Even though what she says may sound completely insane, it usually is the best way to solve my problem. It is these "little" lessons that have played the biggest roll in my life by helping me cope with problems that have come my way.

An anonymous person once quoted, "Experience is a hard teacher. She gives the test first and then the lesson." I understand that I am going to make mistakes for the rest of my life. And I am okay with that! I see each of life's lessons as a new opportunity to be a better person than I was the day before.

—Melissa Monson

Lost Soul

Sometimes I wonder, did I do the right thing? I feel as though I threw my life away. No, I didn't do the right thing. If I did, why am I here behind bars? I lost one of my best friends by doing one stupid little thing. My name is Noah and this is my story.

Ring! "Dude, come on! That's the bell," Trevor yelled. Trevor—my best friend—always freaked out when we were just a minute late for class. We've known each other since first grade and now we were in tenth grade and still the best of friends. After we got in the school building, we raced to our lockers, and I started my combination. Trevor and I always had locker-opening races every morning. Trevor said it fueled our minds for the big day ahead. I never believed in weird stuff like that, but since he did, I just went along with it. My fingers twisted and turned as my mind raced to remember what my combo was in the first place. It's weird how a simple thing like opening your locker every morning can mess you up during the day. I finally got my lock open. I grabbed my history book and swung my head over to see Trevor with his books in his hands, locker closed. I shook my head and laughed. Trevor always beat me during our little races. "Let's go," he said with a smile as we headed down the hallway.

"Man, I have so much homework!" Trevor complained as he and I walked down the street. I nodded in agreement.

"Yeah, I'm bushed," I said with a groan. Out of the corner of my eye I saw him looking at me. He had a worried look on his face. I knew he was wondering why I had my motor cross sweatshirt hood over my head.

"Hey, why do you have your hood up? It's like 77 degrees out here."

"I'm cold," I answered. I wasn't even going to begin to tell him the real reason. He shrugged.

"Anyway, I think I'm just going to skip all that work tonight," I said with a yawn.

"What? Why?" Trevor asked confused. Trevor was a kind of person who always thought homework or school, for that matter, was the key to a good healthy life. I didn't care about any of that stuff.

"I don't know...I'm really tired and plus...my favorite show is on tonight," I said with a little embarrassment.

"You can't keep blowing off your work like that, dude. I always say you only have one life to live, be careful what you do with it. And education is very important to your life!"

"Trevor...you're starting to sound like my mom!" I started to laugh. Trevor always tried to give me speeches about doing my work and stuff.

"Sorry, I'm just trying to help," he stared at the ground.

"That's okay. Hey listen, I have to get home. My mom wants me home early for this family tree project thing she's working on."

"Yeah, well good luck with that!" he said. I laughed and started running down my street corner until I got to the front of my house. I breathed a sigh of relief. The lights in my house were turned off just as I had planned. My mom worked late and wouldn't be home for a couple of hours. I felt bad lying to Trevor, but I couldn't let him find out about my secret. I walked in my house, ran upstairs to my room, and shut the door. I turned to the mirror and put my hood down to reveal the black eye I was hiding from Trevor. It was badly swollen. I ran downstairs to get some ice for it. I rolled my sleeves up to wash my hands. I looked down to see my arms scraped, cut, and bruised. I also had a huge bruise on my back.

These were all wonderful gifts from a guy named Tom Becker, also known as T.B. I never really knew the real reason why he always managed to beat me up or push me around. I guess it was because I was weak. Ever since my dad left, I could never gather my senses. I picked up the ice bag and put it over my eye. It stung badly, but it would heal in a couple days. I always told Trevor about my fights with T.B. He always encouraged me to go tell a teacher, but I always thought that was a bad idea. I was a grown man and I didn't need any help from a teacher, parent, or counselor.

The real reason is that I always told Trevor about my problems, but this time I couldn't, because this time, next time, tomorrow at school would be different. My plan was to use one of my dad's guns to scare T.B. off with. I remember what Trevor said, "You only have one life to live; be careful what you do with it." I knew what I was risking, but I would be careful. It wasn't like I was going to shoot it. Or was I?

It was lunchtime the next day at school, and I knew it would be the perfect time to put my plan to action. I knew Trevor would worry, so I told him I was going for a walk and would be back in a second. I ran outside and spotted T.B. by the school exit. T.B. was with his hang. I walked right up to him. "Hey T.B., what's up?" I said in a sly tone.

"Don't you know?" T.B. replied.

"No sorry. I'm afraid I don't," I held the gun firmly under my jacket.

"Sorry to hear that," he said. He started coming toward me. He got even closer, and I quickly took the gun out and pointed it at him. T.B. stopped in his tracks and stared.

"Noah! What are you doing? Are you crazy! Put the gun down!" I turned to see where the voice was coming from, and there, right behind me, was Trevor. He probably came out looking for me. I stared at him. A look of horror was on his face as his bloodshot eyes started at the gun. T.B. started laughing. Shocked, I shot a glance at T.B. How can he be laughing when I have a gun pointing at him?

"What's so funny?" I asked.

"You," he said. "You're so dramatic. We know you're not going to shoot."

"Oh yeah, well..." I froze. No words came out. I gulped and tried again. "Maybe you should think again," I stopped. There were a hundred different things I could have said better than those five words.

"Wrong answer, Noah." And those were the last words T.B. said when he lunged at me. I heard Trevor's voice yell my name. I fell hard to the floor. The hand holding the gun slammed to the ground firing off three shots. I heard screams in the background. My head banged against the brick wall and knocked me out.

And that's how it happened. I woke up at the police station on a cot with a bandage around my head. A police officer came over and said that I had been knocked out for three hours. I looked around. Everything was blurry, and I was seeing things in double vision. My head spun, and I felt very dizzy. The officer looks at me and told me that two people were killed. T.B. and Trevor were shot and killed that day. As I sit in my little stone prison, I flash back many memories to the time I had the gun pointing at T.B. and the look on Trevor's face when he saw the gun. I bury my face in my hands.

"Kid, it's your dad on the phone."

I looked up to see a guard holding the door open for me. I nodded and got up off my bench. As I headed for the door I remembered: "You only have one life to live, so be careful what you do with it."

—Amanda Grassi

Dewy's Storm Story

Many people tell breathtaking, mind-boggling tales of survival through the harshest weather Mother Nature can yield. My narrative can top them all. And it is not because I have superior story telling capabilities, although I do have an astounding aptitude for that. No, it is the result of living through the most sinister, and the most fabulous, weather.

"How can this be?" some might inquire, "For it seems very unlikely for what you have claimed to be plausible."

Does it though? For I have resided on Earth since the day of its creation, and shall remain here until its destruction.

"Ah, then you are naught but a fairy tale, a legend to entertain children with," some might suggest.

Am I really? For I was confident that I dwell in the realm of reality. You see, I am an element, forceful, and yet soothing. There is not one who has never come in contact with me, yet too many take me for granted. I am water, a droplet named Dewy. During the time of this tale, I was a boy, not young, but not the wisest in some areas.

From the moment I saw him, I wanted to impress him. He was the kind of guy who was always popular, who had a knack for attracting attention. Even the way he calmly looked around was so cool. He acted like he didn't have a care in the world, like he was waiting for someone and they were late, but he did not care; he would just enjoy the scenery. I could picture us being best friends and doing everything together. Even though I entertained myself with images of us being the ones everyone looked up to and admired, I thought that he would never even notice me.

Then he looked my way and smiled. I was sure that he was gazing somewhere over my head, when the thought struck me that he might not know anyone here. I stood there, amazed that someone like him would not have a crowd of friends around him. I waited, positive that he would turn my way again, and sure enough, he glanced at me. I smiled back at him this time and watched, awestruck, as he turned and strode right toward me, like he had planned it the whole time. Yes! He was the one that walked up to me! He picked me out of all the other drops of H2O here!

"Um, hey," he said, almost nervously. I stood there and stared.

Say something! Just act like this happens every day. Yeah, right! Like anyone has ever been the one to introduce himself to me. I have always been the one tagging at someone else's cloud. Shaking these thoughts out of my head, I finally managed to utter a small, "Hi." I silently cursed myself for not having the nerve to say more. But any words of acknowledgement seemed to be enough for him.

He grinned broadly and announced, "My name is Dink. I was separated from some friends of mine while we were falling in the storm yesterday." Oh, so that was why he was by himself. He probably just wanted me to show him the fastest way out of this puddle. He seemed to sense my disappointment. "And I was wondering if I could hang with you, until they arrive. You can come with us when they get here, of course," he began uncertainly.

My face lit up as I exclaimed, "That would be awesome!"

"Great!" Dink said with a smile. "Now what is there to do around here?"

I showed him everything. Although this puddle had only been formed in a storm yesterday, it already had many things to do. We visited the park and played soccer with a small pebble. Then we ate lunch at Puddie's Pizza Place. We went and saw a movie at the Plazma Theater, and munched on popcorn during the film. After that, we went to the Zoo of Plankton. Finally, we ate snow cones as we walked down the street talking about what we had done that day.

"Why is he packing?" Dink asked suddenly. "It can't be time to evaporate yet, can it?"

"I don't think so," I said, and then called, "Sir! Why are you packing?"

"I'm not gonna be the last one out this time," the vender shouted back shaking his finger. "Last time everyone thought that they had out-smarted old Mister Buck and left him behind. But not this time! No way! I'll be the first one out of here this time! You can't play the same trick twice!" At that exact moment, a rock hit his cart. "Lousy hoodlums! I'll get you yet!"

Dewy and I looked up to see three drips running away snickering. The vender was still cursing them madly as we slipped away.

"Paranoid old bat," Dink whispered, "What do you bet I could hit him from here?" Dink jokingly held his snow cone back, as if he were going to chuck it. "Stinking old weather's gone against me too!" he croaked mockingly. We both doubled up with laughter.

"But ya know what?" he said once we had collected ourselves, "We should leave early! Want to?"

"What? Why?" I asked.

"We could leave tomorrow, before the crowd, so that we won't be separated."

"But what about your friends?"

"Oh, they're probably already up there."

So the next morning, we went up to evaporate. Once a vapor, I tried to start a conversation.

"Soooo..." I began, "What's your favorite place in the world?"

—

"Well, Hawaii is beautiful, but I wasn't there for very long. Guess what!"

"What?"

"I witnessed the signing of the Declaration of Independence. Then Jefferson drank me!"

We talked about all the places we'd been and things we'd done. Suddenly, I had a great urge to impress Dink.

"I was on the space shuttle Columbia," I blurted suddenly. Why did I say that? It was not true!

"No way! That's awesome!" Dink said, "What's no gravity like?"

"It's the coolest," I muttered. The rest of the trip up, all Dink talked about was space, and how he hoped to visit it some day. I was quiet most of the time, but Dink did not care. I had an empty feeling in my stomach, and every time Dink said something about the Columbia, I felt I was going to be sick. My stomach was churning and I felt very hot. I could not believe that I had lied! I breathed a sign of relief, when we finally made it up.

"Dink!" someone suddenly yelled.

"Dub!" Dink yelled back, "Hey, Dewy, these are my friends! Dub, Charlie, and Frank, this is Dewy. Told ya they wouldn't wait for me down there!

"Sorry man, we heard that there might be a tornado and wanted to be in the clouds when it happened!" Charlie said.

"Awesome!" Dink said, "I love watching tornadoes from above! It's a good thing I decided to evaporate early."

"Guess what, Dink!" Frank said suddenly.

"What?"

"There is a droplet in this cloud that was on the space shuttle Columbia!" Just my luck. I claim to be on a space ship that I was not on, then I get up here and there is some drop that was actually on it.

"No way!" Dink turned to me. "You can go talk to him! I bet he remembers you! Guys! Dewy here was on the Columbia, too!"

"Nu-uh!"

"How cool!"

"What a oinkydink!"

Suddenly, I felt nauseous. I had to tell the truth or they would find out from the guy who really was on the Columbia. I took a deep breath. Someone was yelling something behind me, but I took no notice. I was going to tell Dink. Dink and his friends were starting to run away, but I grabbed Dink by the shoulder.

"No I wasn't."

'What do you mean? You weren't what? It doesn't matter right now. You need to move!" Dink started to pull me.

"No! I have to tell you now!" I tried to jerk loose, but Dink held tight. For some reason he looked scared.

"Dewy, listen!"

"You listen! I wasn't on the Columbia."

Dink stopped tugging. "What?"

"Dink! Hurry!" Frank yelled. I looked up and saw that he was standing some ten feet away. Someone was still yelling and Dink started to drag me again.

"I made it up. I never even saw the Columbia. I...."

"Tell me later, just..." Dewy began, but I cut him off. The yelling was getting louder.

"I have to tell you now! I wanted you..."

"DEWY!"

"Let me finish!" I was beginning to get annoyed. What was so important that he could not let me finish a single sentence? "I don't know why I..."

"DEWY!!!"

"For falling raindrops, what?!?" I could barely hear him for all the kerfuffle going on behind me.

"You are standing in the middle of the tornado zone!" I looked around. I realized all at once what was going on. The sound I had mistaken for yelling was a siren. Dink's friends had been standing ten feet away on the edge of the gray cloud. Dink and I were standing in the middle of the ominous cloud that was as black as night. As we turned and ran, I felt like everything was in slow motion. When we were half way to the gray cloud, I felt the black giving way behind me. At the same time, Charlie, Dub, Frank, and all started running toward us. I looked back and saw the tornado. I was being sucked into it. Right as I fell, Dink grabbed my hand, but the force knocked him off his feet and we were both falling. We were in the middle of the tornado. Then everything seemed to speed up.

"Dewy! We have to get to the outside!" I nodded

If a drop is ever unfortunate enough to meet a force that is strong enough to pull him apart, he does not die, as most would call it. All his parts turn into what droplets call baby drops. They have no will of their own, until they form together with other baby drops, to make a different drop.

Dink and I struggled and floundered, but we didn't seem to get any closer to getting out. The wind was screaming and laughing at us. It was whipping us around like we were its little toys. My heart was pounding in my head, and the same thought was playing over and over in my mind: we have to make it. I could taste the dirt in my mouth from the tornado. There was a whirl of objects flying around us. We were about to give up, when I saw something. Frank, Charlie, and Dub had made a chain and were reaching their stretched fingertips. One inch closer, two inches closer, slowly we began to move toward them. When we were only one inch away, Dink yelled at me. I looked up and saw a huge limb flying right at us. I swung around it so that Dink might reach Charlie's hand. It worked. We all cheered, but suddenly something hit me full force. Everything went black.

When I came around, I was lying on the ground. There were voices, but at first I could not understand them. Then I remembered what had happened. I sat up so suddenly that I heard someone gasp. Dink, Charlie, Frank, and Dub were all standing around me. Even though most of them looked pretty banged up, they were all grinning from ear to ear.

"You know what, Dink?" Frank started, "We are gonna make sure any new friends you have are smart enough to realize when they are standing in the middle of a tornado zone."

"All because you weren't on Space Shuttle Columbia, and you couldn't wait one more second to tell Dink," Dub chuckled.

"I'm really, really sorry, Dink! I should have been paying attention." I looked down.

"Don't worry about it," Dink said.

"I'll never lie again!" I whispered miserably.

"Yeah," Charlie said, "because you know if you do, then you'll be sucked up by a tornado!"

We all laughed and had a great time chatting animatedly about out experience that taught us all a lesson: Don't lie!

—Joslyn Arthur

Come Spring, Come

Wind is rising,
While she waits,
"Come Spring, come," she calls.
Wind only whistles.
"Tell me Wind," she commands,
"When is Spring coming?"
Wind whistles louder this time,
"Soon," Wind says, "Soon."
She looks outside and waits,
She waits long, so long.
She longs for Spring to come.
A tear rolls down her cheek.
"Is Spring here?" she calls to Wind.
"Almost," Wind says, "Almost."

Wind got softer, the girl could tell.
She looked out the window and there,
There it was, the sign,
The sign that said Winter was gone.
She ran outside and then, only then,
Beautiful Robin perched on her shoulder.
"Spring is here, it is,"
He whispered in her ear.
More tears fell from her cheek
As she twirled and landed in the grass.
"Thank you Wind, thank you."

—Kayla Horseman

Letter of Reconciliation

Dear Friend,

You were there at my ninth birthday party, and we laughed together, as though nothing could ever separate us. We went to the zoo together and went apple picking. Remember when we could not find the cheetahs, and they were right in front of us? At that point, I thought that neither friends, boys, or even time could separate us.

Time went on, and we grew further away from one another. You had your friends, and I had mine. Except for the occasional "hello" in the hall, we did not talk like we used to. Then things got worse; at lunch you and your friends would make fun of me, or just completely ignore me.

Some days, when we were alone, you would talk to me, and make me feel on top of the world. But on those days that you would make fun of me, I would bleed with an inner pain that would not go away.

I am writing you this letter to tell you how I feel, so that you will not hurt me again. A few weeks ago, I told you how I felt, and I think that you have done a better job of just caring for me. We might not be friends forever, but your friendship means a lot to me right now. I hope that you read this letter and learn my true feelings for you. No matter what happens, I will always value and cherish the memories we have had together.

Sincerely,
Christine Temple

An Angel From Above

I have this guy-friend named Ian. I love him as a brother, but a few months ago, I thought of him as the biggest crush that I have ever had in my preteen life. I have known him for about three years, when our relationship flipped upside-down! His family and my family would usually meet at the lake for parties. Before his accident, he loved to play football, wrestle, kneeboard, and wakeboard.

On an icy day in January, Ian went out and got the mail. On his way back to his house, he slipped and fell on the ice, and hit the side of his head. I was online about an hour later when his dad was on, so I talked to him. I asked him what Ian was doing, and he told me that he was at the hospital. I did not know about what had happened just an hour earlier. Jokingly, I said, "What, to work out?" Ian usually went to the hospital to work out. He told me what happened to his son, out on the slippery ice. I felt so stupid, and so scared, because I was clueless.

No one knew what Ian's conditions were. All I knew was that he was at the hospital, getting x-rays and running complicated tests. I would call or get online to try to talk to them, but no one was home. About a week after his big fall, my mom called their house. His mom answered, and, as it turns out, tomorrow would be Ian's birthday. We went to his favorite Chinese restaurant, China Garden. There I found out that he had a cyst. I had no idea what a cyst was. A cyst basically is just a pocket of fluid that was cutting off Ian's blood supply to his brain.

Ian was going to have a rare brain surgery in a matter of two months. I was so scared! If that doctor did one thing wrong, Ian could die or be a vegetable for the rest of his life! Every time I came around him, he never talked much. As it turns out, he was scared, too. He did not want to die; he was only fourteen!

It was Labor Day weekend, and Ian was having his surgery on Tuesday. Something unexpected happened to him over the weekend. The day before he had his surgery, he went streaking in the woods with his cousin! When he was being prepped for surgery, they found poison ivy all over his body. He also had a terrible sunburn all over. The doctor said to give him three shots to put him out cold.

Ian's surgery was set for seven a.m., but his surgery was delayed, until one p.m. I was at a soccer camp all day long, and as soon as I got out, I rushed over to the hospital to find out that he had just made it into recovery. The next day, my mom and I went to see Ian. Right when we walked into his room, he was sitting up watching golf and eating a box of chocolates! I was so happy he was okay, even though he had seventeen stitches on the left side of his head! I do not know what I would've done without him.

—Lauryn Young

PERSHING MIDDLE SCHOOL

Scorpion

Nearly four years ago I was stung by a scorpion. This encounter happened so rapidly that the pain is all I can recall. The searing, murderous pain was awful, but it has inspired me to write this story. So, join me at my grandparents' house out in the middle of nowhere.

After dinner one night I was barefooted (a huge mistake), and I sauntered happily to the living room. Then, suddenly, a blazing nail was thrust into my big toe. Through tears, I stumbled and fell on the nearby couch, thinking that I had stepped on a staple sticking up from the carpet. I glanced back and saw the most hideous thing skitter across the brown floor, the very thing that I had tread on. It blended in perfectly with the old rug.

I screamed about "a beetle" as my concerned family gathered around. At the time I didn't know what the revolting assassin was, so I labeled it "the beetle."

When my account was understood, an ointment was applied, and "the beetle" taken care of. Apparently, as my foot hovered over the scorpion, it had stung me for demented defense purposes. My grandparents then informed me that the scorpion hadn't been fatal or even harmful (sure...), and they were as common in Oklahoma as kids with braces. So, the lesson is, do not have carpet that can camouflage wicked things that sting and run, and wear shoes at all times when in country homes!

—Lane Pybas

The Heart of a President

Have you ever thought of being President? I have. I ran for President of Student Council at Cowden Elementary. Running for President is not as easy as it sounds. It's a real exercise of the heart. From writing, and giving the speech, to listening for the results, my heart felt many different emotions, and beat at many different speeds.

The first thing I had to do was write a speech convincing people to vote for me. I knew I couldn't lie to people in my speech, so I didn't make any promises I couldn't keep. I did promise I would try to make school fun, because I love to have fun! I gave examples of how I had helped people at Cowden, and that I would give special help to the kindergartners. I had been at Cowden since kindergarten, and it had a special place in my heart.

The day came to give our speeches. I had to wait on the stage until my turn. My feet were tapping, I was clenching my hands, and my heart was beating a mile a minute. I was third in line, and all the third through fifth graders were watching. I slowly walked to the podium. I could feel my heart beating on the outside. I pulled all the courage I had in my heart, and started to talk. I don't even remember speaking, but I can remember the clapping when I was done.

I had to wait two days before the results of the election were announced. They told us the announcements would come over the intercom. My teacher told us not to yell out. I had settled back into school, and the excitement of giving the speeches was over, but when I heard the click of the speaker, my heart stopped. I knew I would soon hear the results. When I heard, "The President for the 2003 school year is Brett Moore," my heart was screaming inside. But then I saw my friends, who didn't win, with tears in their eyes, and my heart felt sorry for them.

Still, I knew my mom had heard the great news over the intercom in her 2nd grade room, and her heart was full of pride. My heart was beating rapidly with excitement, and then I realized I was now the Student Council President, and I had better get to work. It was time to get down to the heart of the matter.. .leading the people who had voted for me, and starting to have fun!

—Brett Moore

If you liked this book, check out *Voices from the Middle: Stepping out into the real world*, Book One. You can get it at a bookstore near you.

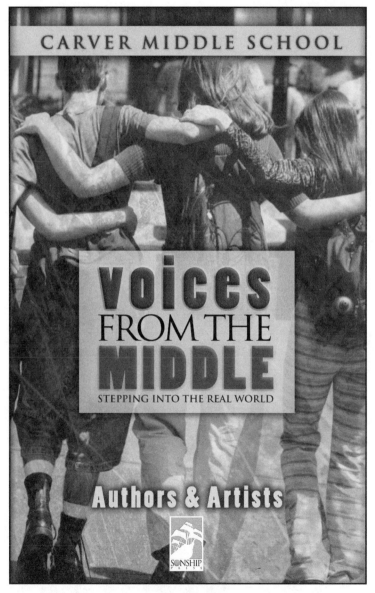